"WOW! This is a must read! Give yourself a present and take time to read *Permission to Win*! It can fuel your dream ... !"

Patricia Fripp
Author, *Insights Into Excellence*

"*Permission to Win* delivers the goods! It's a terrific motivational lift as well as a complete program for those who want to win in every facet of their lives. Want to give your spirits a boost? Start your day by reading a chapter of Ray Pelletier's book instead of the morning paper!"

Michael LeBoeuf
Author, *Working Smart; The Perfect Business*

"*Permission to Win* is sure to be a classic. I couldn't keep the manuscript in my hands ... they were passing it around the office! I love the stories, and the message is priceless! ... *Permission to Win* is the first step to a lifetime of 'better than terrific days!' "

T. Scott Gross
Author, *Positively Outrageous Service*

"This book is MUST reading for anyone who wants to live a richer and happier life! Ray lays it out in plain language, smooth style, and deep conviction. His advice is sound, practical, and proven. Highly recommended."

Nido R. Qubein
Author, *How to Be a Great Communicator*

"When Ray Pelletier speaks at conventions and management meetings, people are entranced by his message and delivery. They hang on his every word—and idea. They are transformed. Reading *Permission to Win*, I was struck by how clearly the writing is just like his speaking!"

Roger E. Herman, CSP, CMC
Author, *Futurist*

"The message is powerful ... What a great revelation! Thanks, Ray!"

Ty Boyd
Author, *Visions—From the Leaders of Today for the Leaders of Tomorrow*

"Reading Ray's Book, *Permission to Win*, was like attending a private lecture by Ray himself. If you didn't believe in yourself before you read the book, you most certainly absolutely have to believe in you now!"

Bert Hammel
Head Basketball Coach, Merrimack College

"In *Permission to Win*, Ray Pelletier shows you how to eliminate self-doubt and focus on accomplishing your mission. Heed ... and find it works! I loved it!"

Jim Tunney, Ed.D.
Professional speaker and former NFL referee

"If you have ever asked yourself, 'How will I get through one more day and come out of the darkness into the light,' Pelletier's passion will light a fire under you! ... Pelletier's personal pizzazz and sharing from the gut will get you to finally take action in your quest to turn dreams into realities!"

Rosita Perez, CPAE
President, Creative Living Programs, Inc.

"You certainly have my permission to read *Permission to Win*! In fact, consider it an order if you're interested in a powerful coach for your personal life and career! A constant motivational companion. It's like having a coaching staff, cheerleaders, and fans at your side all the time!"

> Alan Weiss, Ph.D.
> Author, *Million Dollar Consulting*

"This book on goals and winning is a winner in every respect. It will make a difference in the lives of so many people."

> Cavett Robert
> Founder and Chairman Emeritus,
> National Speakers Association

"Ray Pelletier is a champion in every aspect of his life. Now I know why. This magnificent book will fire up the hearts of all who read it!"

> Dottie Walters
> President, Walters International Speakers Bureau
> Publisher, *Sharing Ideas* (Speakers News Magazine)

"Ray Pelletier is a winner—he has coached winners on and off athletic fields. In this book, he not only gives the reader permission to win, he titillates the soul with his stories while providing specific, action steps that are proven by experience. Read this book!"

Dennis McCuistion
Strategist and PBS Talk-Show Host

"Ray Pelletier's *Permission to Win* is a challenge to a life of winning through giving! A reflection of a walk that talks! This is a must-read life manual by an incredible fellow traveler!"

Naomi Rhode, CSP, CPAE
Author, *More Beautiful Than Diamonds*

"Going from zero to infinity isn't meant to be an easy task, but Ray helps everyone to discover the key within themselves to enter the adventure."

Jeff Herman, President,
The Jeff Herman Literary Agency

"Self-esteem—the vital ingredient to success. Ray Pelletier, with this book, seeks out the sleeping giant within us and gives to the reader the keys to self-esteem. We will rise no higher than the expectations we have for ourselves. Low expectations of others is the reason for the failure of welfare. We must believe in the strength of the human spirit, as does Ray Pelletier in this book!"

> E. Clay Shaw, Jr.
> Member of Congress

"Ray Pelletier walks his talk. He is truly 'America's Attitude Coach,' with a string of successful ventures with a wide variety of clients. This book brings it all together in an entertaining and inspiring manner. Read it! Enjoy it! And win!"

> George Morrisey, CSP, CPAE
> Author, *Creating Your Future; Personal Strategic Planning for Professionals*

"*Permission to Win* is more than a book. It's a way of life. Ray Pelletier shows you that you can live a full life regardless of your circumstances. The secret is in your attitude."

> Gregory J. P. Godek
> Author, *1001 Ways To Be Romantic*

"...entertaining, uplifting, and positive!"

Tom Osborne
Head Football Coach
University of Nebraska

"This book is powerful and will affect the bottom line in your personal and business life. With this terrific tool, you will receive a high return on investment."

Somers H. White
President, Somers White Company,
Management and Financial Consultants

Permission to Win

Permission to Win

by

Ray Pelletier

Oakhill Press
Akron, Ohio • New York

Permission to Win

Library of Congress Cataloging-in-Publication Data

Pelletier, Ray, 1948-
    Permission to win / by Ray Pelletier.
    ISBN 1-886939-10-1 (hardcover)
    1. Success-Psychological aspects.   I. Title.
BF637.S8P44   1996   96-8180
158--dc20   CIP

0 9 8 7 6 5 4 3 2 1

First Printing, January 1, 1997

RAY PELLETIER is an international world-class business speaker and the founder and president of The Pelletier Group, an organization founded on the very simplest of principles: to bring out the champion that truly resides in every human spirit. Ray recognizes no exception to that principle—every man and woman, in every walk of life and under any circumstance, has it within themselves to be unconquerable.

With a personal dynamism, conviction, and persuasiveness that has been termed "electrifying," (*Successful Meetings* magazine calls him "a new breed of motivator"), Ray Pelletier has been invited to speak before a long list of major corporations and sports teams such as AT&T; Disney Productions; GTE; Erickson; Junior Chamber International; and the football teams at the University of Notre Dame, University of Nebraska, USC, and for the Miami Hurricanes (to give you just a small sampling from the list). He has a real passion for youth and has addressed thousands of college and high-school students at schools and conferences as well as in special programs addressing family matters and the problems of those who are seriously ill, troubled, or handicapped.

While all of Ray's speaking programs are precisely tailored and exhaustively researched* to assure the motivational result most needed by the particular audience he's addressing, the bottom line of his messages is invariably the same: there is an absolute necessity to give yourself permission to win, to recognize and bring out the champion inside of yourself and to approach every day of your life as January 1st—the day that you WILL BE that champion.

To Ray Pelletier, "America's Business Attitude Coach," today is your January 1st. This is the day you become a winner. This is the day you give yourself permission to win. And it will be the same each day hereafter. There's no nonsense about it. Those aren't just words. Ray Pelletier is real life. Today IS the day! You'll see.

---

*Ray Pelletier is widely recognized for having done the definitive research on Attitude and Team Development. In a ten-year study, he researched in depth one of the nation's largest companies, analyzing their 30 profit centers. He took this data and tested his findings against 300 different companies and over 30 different sports teams. By sharing this data with clients and cross-referencing it with his own research into the client organization, he is able to determine the strengths and weaknesses within that organization and provide the specific tools that will enable the client's people to outperform the competition.

Permission to Win

CONTENTS

ACKNOWLEDGMENTS

I am so fortunate to have so many people to thank. The following list is by no means complete, but it starts where it should start—with you, the reader. If you've wondered whether an author would ever think enough of you to say *"THANK YOU!"*, you can stop wondering. This book is for YOU.

Joyce, my best friend, my love, my soul-mate.

My Mom, who taught me about love; Dad, who was a real subliminal motivator and encouraged me to go to Toastmasters. They both live in Heaven and I miss them terribly. I know they would love this book.

Each of my brothers, who have affected me in significant ways. Thanks to Phil, Bill, Jere, and Lee.

Zoraida, for helping me grow up, believing in me, and for giving me our children.

Kim and Ray, for the joy you bring into my life.

The Pelletier Group Team and all who have worked with me throughout all these years, especially Fred Bell. A great big THANK YOU.

The members of the National Speakers Association. Especially Naomi Rhode for believing in me when I thought no one else did.

Meeting Planners, who have chosen me to speak for their companies and associations. I am so grateful.

Special coaches, who allowed me in their locker rooms.

The Breakfast Club, for keeping me humble, and for just being there.

And most important, to my God—for allowing me the *"privilege of the platform"*—and without whom neither this book nor any acknowledgment nor anything else could be accomplished.

A NOTE OF SPECIAL APPRECIATION TO THE CELEX GROUP, INC.

Without exception, the quotes at the bottom of the pages in this book are taken from the superb motivational book, *THE EDGE*, Copyright © 1983, 1986, and 1990 by Howard E. Ferguson. All quotations are *used with permission and published by Celex Group, Inc./Celebrating Excellence, all rights reserved.* Their permission to use the quotes from *THE EDGE* has added greatly to the flavor of this manuscript.

DEDICATION

Dedicated to my soul-mate, Joyce, and to my family and close friends, for the inspiration and support I have received from them. And to my parents, who now live in Heaven, for the love and "permission to win" they gave me. They have all touched my life positively.

Thank you!

FOREWORD

Like Ray, I believe each person reading this book has the potential to be a true champion. Ray Pelletier is world-class in giving people permission to win.

As you may know, my acronym for *"win"* is **W**hat's **I**mportant **N**ow. What I think is important now is that you take some time to read this book and to truly give yourself permission to win and take your game to the next level.

I've enjoyed working with Ray. He's a true professional, on the platform and off, and I promise you that if you invest time in reading this book, you'll experience a life that is loaded with winning moments.

Best wishes,

LOU HOLTZ
Head Football Coach,
University of Notre Dame

INTRODUCTION

Many years ago, I sat in a first-grade classroom waiting for a gold star being handed out by Mrs. Lemon. It was a reward for our very first assignment, and she came to each desk, saying to each student, *"Congratulations; here's your star."* Desk by desk she came, a smile on her face: *"Congratulations; here's your star."*

But there was to be no star for me. When she reached my desk, her smile changed to a scowl and she threw my paper at me. In a voice clearly heard by all, she said: *"I don't know what's wrong with you! You're just not as smart as your brothers!"*

There was nothing wrong with my paper and I hadn't acted up in Mrs. Lemon's class or done anything that would have even brought me to her attention, let alone cause her to embarrass me like that. I've never been able to understand it—and her strange malevolence persisted as the months went by. Every day, in one way or another, she continued to tear me down in front of the class, as if I were the personification of some hated thing in her past.

At the end of that year, she called me to the front of the class, pointed her finger at me and said: *"I told you you weren't as smart as your brothers. Now you go back to your seat. You're not going to pass first grade. You've failed."*

That first year in school was a defining one for me—you can believe it. Every chance she got, Mrs. Lemon, the reigning authority for thirty kids, made sure they understood that I was worthless. That I was a failure. She pounded it into them as thoroughly as she taught them to read. The class believed it.

And by the end of the year, I believed it. I pretended that I was okay ... that nothing bothered me. But I wasn't okay at all.

For whatever warped reason, that first-grade teacher had programmed me to believe I was a loser—and that was exactly how I acted, hating school authority, repeating seventh grade, graduating by the absolute minimum margin, and facing life with very low self-esteem ...

... until I grew up enough to understand what had happened to me.

I don't know exactly when I revolted against Mrs. Lemon's programming—it was sometime in my early twenties—but I do know that the revolt came suddenly, without a moment's thinking about it, and that it came with a vengeance.

No mental struggle was involved in this revolt. No long walks in the woods pondering the meaning of life. No soulful discussions with friends or counselors. That wasn't my style. I had developed a loser's mentality and that was that—good at sports and raising hell, but I wasn't going anywhere important and I'd become accustomed to thinking about myself that way and taking things as they came without worrying about it.

So, that was my mindset, and the only lead-up to the coming revolt was a vague dissatisfaction with things. More and more each day, I had been coming to resent the idea that I was a loser. I was accustomed to that role, as I said, but it was becoming increasingly uncomfortable. It wasn't anything I really thought about. It was just there ... making me uneasy ... nagging at me. It was subliminal, but it was persistent, sort of simmering away quietly on a burner in the back of my mind.

And then, in one sudden moment, the revolt came.

Out of the blue one day, and totally unexpectedly (I think I was just walking along the street), my heart and head suddenly told me, as plainly as if they had spoken to me, that as of that instant enough had become enough. Not for a second longer was I to allow myself to tolerate self-doubt and self-pity, nor any notion whatever that I was a loser. Not for one more second. *I was better than that!*

It was more than a thought; it was a command from somewhere inside me. It couldn't have been more compelling if it had been engraved on a stone tablet and handed to me, and I knew exactly what I had to do. Faster than I can say it, I reached into myself, pulled the handle, and flushed Mrs. Lemon and all the yesterdays and all the negative programming and all the self-doubts out of my system.

Just like that.

Before I'd taken the next step along that street, the past was over. There were no second thoughts. No qualifications. Ray Pelletier, the loser, no longer existed. And when I say it happened just as fast as that, I mean it happened <u>exactly</u> as fast as that.

In that second, I immediately stepped into the first day of a new life wholly convinced that I was a winner.

The change was to be as permanent as it was immediate, and in time I came to give that moment a name. I called it my "January 1st," and it had come with a permit — the *permission to win.*

Aside from my faith in God and my family, that permission—which I gave to myself on that street—was by far the greatest gift I have ever received. It's worked wonders for me in every area of my life, both personal and business; it has consistently enabled me to overcome feelings of inadequacy and doubt; it gave me the courage to exchange a dull, so-so career for one of dynamism, fulfillment, and considerable financial success; it has brought me back from big-time personal grief; it enables me to see every problem as an opportunity—whatever the problem may be and from wherever it may come—and to approach it in a positive, competitive, and confident manner with <u>winning</u> instinctively and automatically <u>assured</u> to me in my mind. And that, friends, is 99% of the struggle involved in winning.

The world is full of Mrs. Lemons. It's full of circumstances engineered to make us feel incompetent and inadequate and convince us that we're losers. It's full of broken marriages, failed relationships, unfulfilled careers, dead-end jobs, and success that never comes. Let's face it: the big-time reality of the 20th century isn't jets and computers; it's millions of people consulting books like this one to see if there isn't some way, some formula, to improve their lives.

As "America's Attitude Coach," I spend my working life addressing all kinds of audiences—prisoners who think they're without hope, kids with cancer, and (on the other end of the scale) some of the most "successful" and accomplished people in the world: athletes, champions, CEOs, and other people in all walks of life who seem to have everything together ... everything most of us dream about. Yet, these audiences share a common need, and there I am, speaking to them all, asked to provide that magic "something" that will assure them of winning.

The truth of it is that there's nothing magic about it at all. The formula for winning in life, whether you're in jail or in chemotherapy or in a championship locker-room or in the executive suite, is intuitive and instinctive. It's within every one of us, and the purpose of this book is to show you how to use and master it. When you gain that mastery, it will result in a fundamental change in the way you think—so fundamental that it will affect your approach to every challenge and problem life throws at you, enabling you to take charge of your life in a way that should be infinitely more positive and fulfilling than anything you've ever imagined.

That's a big order to be filled by a small book.

But—as I told a locker-room full of huge, sweaty Notre Dame football players, none of whom knew me and all of whom were eying me narrowly—*"Fellas, I believe in you and I want you to be the champions God made you to be, and that's why I'm here. Just give me your attention for a little bit ... ."*

They did ... and they won the Orange Bowl (21-6) ... and Lou Holtz presented me with the game ball for giving his team *permission to win.*

I believe in you, I want you to be a winner, and that's why I'm here. Just give me your attention for a little bit ...

At the end of this book, you'll be asked to take five seconds to go to a mirror and tell yourself, loudly and firmly: "**I give you permission to win.**"

It is not a trivial request. It will be a serious act of baptism into a new belief in yourself—and it is an act your mind will never let you forget.

You're not ready for it yet.

But you will be by the time you've finished reading.

1

TALKING WITH CHAMPIONS

Every audience I speak to is a championship audience. In an average week, I'll address 1,500 people or more in my seminars and speaking engagements—in places ranging from inner-city slums to Fortune 500 offices—and it's taught me that every human being is born with the ability to overcome the problems and obstacles fate throws at them. I haven't met one person who doesn't have that inherent champion's capacity. Not one.

It doesn't matter where you may be in your life. It doesn't matter who you are or what troubles you have. It doesn't matter if you're black or white, homeless, locked away in prison or brought up in a ghetto or a castle. It doesn't matter if your business or marriage has just failed or if you have been diagnosed with a terminal disease. It truly doesn't matter. There is a champion inside you that cannot be defeated. If you're alive, that champion is in there. It's built into your spirit. You didn't put it there. You didn't create it. It was given to you at birth. It's part of you.

Whether I'm facing you in a seminar or talking with you from these pages, that champion is the only thing I see. And I can tell you this—it's the best raw material any coach could ask for.

So, that's where I start—knowing you're a champion—and I'm counting on you to work with me to bring that champion out into the open so you can realize your full potential as a winner.

I'll give you the best I have. Give me the same, and I promise you we'll be successful.

When I look around at the world, the thing I see most clearly is the terrible harm people do to themselves by failing to recognize their inbuilt winner's potential. They focus on their failures and judge themselves accordingly, never allowing the champion to emerge. They refuse to give themselves permission to win, and it is a tragic and ruinous waste.

Winning is a <u>birthright</u>—and a person's failure to recognize this and apply a positive winner's attitude in his or her life can rob them of happiness, success, health, and progress. Negativity and self-pity can turn the grief of a broken marriage into a lifelong retreat from happiness. It makes people in critically poor health give up and submit to their situation, stripping away their opportunity to be mentally victorious and to enjoy life despite their illness. Negative thinking can stop a child's potential in its tracks. Negativity denies legions of adults the ability to be more productive and valuable to their employers and to go forward in their careers (a topic I'm continually invited to address, not only in American business seminars, but around the world).

Many, many books have been authored on the subject of negativity, and many, many solutions are offered, but it continues to be the central malady of our society.

I believe the number one influence that sabotages people's success and happiness is their preoccupation with their failures and with the miserable circumstances in which they find themselves. They give up. They convince themselves that they can't get through their problems, that they can't win, that they don't have the stuff of champions. It's the great lie they tell themselves behind their masks of self-pity.

I know. I've been there. I'm probably a bigger failure than anyone reading this book. I've fallen on my face so many times it would take another book to record it all. You name the area—business, family, financial— and I've failed in it. And I mean *seriously* failed.

In the early days of my business, I had my telephone service cut off so often it became routine—and yet, a few years later, I was giving seminars to telephone executives.

I've had a marriage fail, I've been on my death-bed, I've lost loved ones—and yet, today, I'm asked to encourage thousands of people in similar situations.

There's a tremendous amount of big-time pain and confusion out there. Gentle, wonderful, caring people are being hammered to the ground by fate and circumstance. Bright, talented, deserving men and women are unable to advance in their careers. Everywhere I look, people are unhappy, dismayed, confused. Somewhere in their past they've had a Simon (as in the game Simon Says)—a negative-thinking Simon that subtly programmed them to give in to problems and adversities. A Simon that caused them to focus on what they <u>can't</u> do rather than what they <u>can</u> do. The result is that they don't have the will to walk away from their failures. They're more concerned about their embarrassment than their dreams. They're continually beating themselves up. They have little or no confidence or sense of self-worth. Simon says, *"give up"* ... and they give up.

Who's the Simon in <u>your</u> life? Who programmed you? You need to know. You need to deal with it. You need to replace that old Simon with the champion inside you. I don't care how strong an influence the old Simon has had on you. I don't care whether the Simon in your life is a person or a circumstance. Whoever or whatever it is, the champion in you is stronger. A *lot* stronger. But you have to stop holding him back. You have to give that champion a chance to emerge and take charge of your life.

For many years, I've known that my mission is to touch people's lives positively—to enable them to be the winners they really are. When you get to Chapter 4, Goals and Missions, you'll see that you also have a mission. It may not be the same as mine. But it will have the same kind of foundation. It will be based on who you really are and on the unique talents and interests that enable you to be of valuable service to yourself and to the world.

Your mission will be to pursue the dream you instinctively want to fulfill and know that you should and can fulfill. This isn't something you invent or contrive. *Your mission is the voice of the champion inside you.* It's always there, talking to you. It knows what's best for you, what you were *meant* to do. This is the right Simon in your life, as it is in mine. This is the Simon you'll discover for yourself. It is genuine. Honest. Positive. Capable. It is the voice of an overcomer. It is generous. Forgiving. Compassionate. Truly caring. It focuses you on fulfilling the dreams that give your life purpose, and on helping others fulfill their own dreams.

All told, it is the voice of a winner. It's coming from inside you and cries to be heard.

That's why I'm here—to help you hear it, act on it, and be the champion you really are.

2

DECIDE TO WIN

The first step in winning is to <u>decide</u> to win. *"Not to decide is to decide."*

The second step is to <u>expect</u> to win.

Expect this book to show you how to be a winner. Expect to become that champion. There's nothing complicated about it. There's no reason to hold back. Just decide and <u>expect</u> it.

I expect to win. I expect you to change your life. I expect to hear from you telling me what a difference my coaching has made in your life. I expect some of you to say, *"Ray, you're the first one who ever called me a winner. You made me decide. That was the start I needed."*

I expect others to tell me: *"Thanks for the book. I've achieved some of my goals, but the ones I want most have always eluded me. Now I know why. I can't believe how much I've held myself back over all these years. I can't believe how I constantly sabotaged myself. I can't believe I never gave myself permission to win. I just didn't get it."*

Expect to "get it." Expect to win. Do that, and you're halfway to your goal of being a winner in every area of your life.

So just do it. Decide. I'm counting on it. And bear one great truth in mind: winning is a decision. It's conscious. It's deliberate. You decide to win or you let fate decide it for you. Either way, your decision dictates the way you play the game of life and how it turns out.

Deciding you're a winner may be a strange thought to you. It's a champion's thought. You may not be used to it. But try it on now—let the champion in you emerge by deciding that this book will change your life and make you a winner. Be confident. Expect it. Decide. As I said, that decision is half the journey to becoming a winner. The second half of the journey is just a matter of learning how to apply your decision to win in every area of your life.

Have you decided? I believe you have. Why wouldn't you? I can't imagine anything else. So, now that we're all thinking in terms of winning, let's get on with the journey.

Many years ago, there was a great magician and escape artist. His name was Erich Weiss. To give a demonstration of his artistry, he allowed himself to be put in a jail cell from which he said he would escape in twenty minutes. The constable closed the door of the cell and the twenty minutes started.

At the end of that time, he hadn't escaped. For the first time in his career, Erich Weiss—known to the world as Houdini—had failed. But he was a pro and he stayed in that cell for seven and a half hours before he finally called out, *"I quit!"* The constable walked over, put his hand on the big iron door and just pulled it open. The cell door had never been locked. It was only locked in Houdini's mind!

That's not going to happen to you. As of right now, the door to your mind is no longer locked. Just by reading this, you're opening your mind to a new way of thinking that will allow you to get out of the cells you're in. Just by reading this, you're giving yourself permission to win and you're starting to rid yourself of the old mind-sets that inhibit you from winning.

You've only covered a few pages, but no matter what problems are in your life at this moment you're already starting to sense a possible new way of facing them—with a winning attitude. That attitude can't be avoided—not when you're reading this book. It's happening. You know it and I know it. Look at your calendar. Cross out the date and put in a new one. This is your January 1st—the day you've already started to restructure your thinking to escape from every cell in which life has confined you. This is the day you've given yourself *permission to win.*

What kind of cell are you in? Have you just found out you have AIDS? Or cancer? Have you just lost your job? Is your marriage in trouble? Did someone you love die? Do you lack confidence and self-esteem? Are you depressed? Have you been convicted of a crime and sent to jail? Are you out of money?

Life is full of such prisons—some of them we construct for ourselves; some of them life deals to us. Some of them are big-time, high-security prisons, such as cancer; some of them are low-security prisons, such as dissatisfaction with our job, or not knowing who we really are, or never quite achieving the success we've hoped for. The way out of <u>all</u> of these cells—the way to overcome the effects of <u>every</u> circumstance of life and change things around and emerge as victors—is wholly, totally, exclusively within our own heads. You are the only one who can give yourself *permission to win.* You are the only one who has the master key to your prison. You are allowed one phone call when you're put in prison, and you <u>must</u> make that call to yourself!

Let me tell you about the greatest group of winners I ever met. Every one of them was in a high-security prison, every one of them made that phone call to themselves, every one of them gave themselves permission to win—and every one of them is a winner.

One of my most satisfying and important goals every year is to speak with kids at cancer camps—ages range from 8 to 18. It's amazing to be with these youngsters and see how their spirits have won out over their pain and terrible circumstances. I perform magic for them, play some games, and then I invariably gather them around at one point—some of them sitting, some of them lying on the floor from recent chemotherapy—and I ask them why they're <u>glad</u> they have cancer.

For forty-five minutes, these wonderful young people will give me their answers:

"I'm glad I have cancer because I get to go to camp."

"I have a better relationship with my folks."

"I understand more about the medical field."

"It's made me love everybody who is sick."

An 18-year-old says: *"I'm glad I have cancer because I appreciate life more than I ever did before. I know how to use and treasure every minute of it."*

One after the other they'll speak, a few of them barely able to move. It's extraordinary. Compelling. And if you think such a session would give you pain and sorrow, I tell you it would give you the opposite. You would experience wonder and joy and hope at this amazing display of indomitable human spirit. Nowhere else in my travels have I met winners such as these! In every way, they have overcome the cruelest of situations and emerged victorious! And how? They have the right attitude and they have given themselves permission to win!

Now what is that terrible problem you think <u>you</u> have?

Wherever you are in your life, regardless of how bewildered or hurt you may be, however lost you may feel and whatever your circumstances, few of you will be able to say that your situation is worse than it is for these beautiful youngsters in the cancer camps. They provide you with a reality check—placing a relative value on that seemingly hopeless place you think you're in at the moment. Those young people worked their way out of their hopelessness by refusing to give in, by challenging their circumstances, by thinking of things in new terms, and by giving themselves permission to score a victory over their situation. Nobody else gave them that permission. They gave it to themselves.

So can you.

Today. *Right now!*

Giving yourself permission to win also gives your self-esteem permission to operate positively. This is important, and it belongs right up front in this book.

Low self-esteem is a big-time handicap. It's also a big-time business. Hundreds of books are published every year telling us how to acquire high self-esteem, but the truth of it is that we already have all the self-esteem available to us that we can use.

When you were a kid, did somebody ever accuse you of being stupid and worthless or something else equally negative—the way I was accused by my first-grade teacher, Mrs. Lemon? Unless you grew up on another planet, it's happened to you—maybe it wasn't a teacher, maybe it was someone else—but I guarantee your subconscious mind has never forgotten it. Your immediate reaction was probably a combination of anger, hurt, and defensiveness. You knew you weren't worthless.

That's high self-esteem in action. It's instinctive. We all have it. God gave it to us. We've just allowed the Mrs. Lemons of this world to beat it down so much that we can't find it.

Self-esteem has been defined in countless ways. My definition is this: **"If you respect yourself, regardless of what others may think of you, you have high self-esteem."** The essential word is "self"—it's your respect for yourself that is at issue—and once you've regained it, you are armed with the most powerful weapon ever devised against the problems that life programs for you.

How do you regain your self-esteem? You do it by giving yourself *permission to win* ... by thinking of yourself as a winner. The moment you do that, you suddenly allow your self-esteem to operate; you go forward with confidence, self-respect, and the sure knowledge that you can overcome your problems. Those are the attitudes that define high self-esteem. They come automatically when you give yourself permission to win.

Most people's self-esteem is superficial. It can be destroyed by a look, the loss of a job, a broken marriage, or by the low opinion others may have of them. It can bring them to terrible places of unhappiness and misery, offering them neither the will nor the way to escape. This sort of self-esteem is celluloid rather than ivory, and there is no strength in it, no integrity to withstand disaster. It's based on transitory things that are subject to change by outside forces—our financial status, our job—and when these things collapse, so does the self-esteem. Those who lean on this sort of self-esteem are financing themselves with fool's gold rather than with the genuine article, and it will be valueless when tested. It is not the mark of a winner.

<u>Real</u> self-esteem is based on the truth of who you are—the uniqueness that makes you worthwhile—and when your self-esteem is based on that solid foundation of truth, it is truly indestructible. The world may obliterate everything else in your life, but your self-esteem will stand, giving you the will and the reason to go on and win. This isn't the kind of self-esteem that can be controlled by outside forces. It is founded on the truth you've recognized within yourself and is controlled by that truth. It is not subject to the whims of fate. It cannot be mastered by circumstances. It is known only to you and belongs only to you. It gives you a permanently positive attitude—an unshakable conviction of self-worth—that enables you to survive, to find meaning in your existence, to go forward in your life and change terrible situations into personal victory.

That's the kind of <u>real</u> self-esteem you can expect when you give yourself permission to win. The two go hand-in-hand. It's instinctive and automatic.

Consider this carefully: the moment you give yourself permission to win—the moment you start to think of yourself as a winner—you automatically begin to focus on the special truths about yourself that will enable you to win, and these are the very truths that give rise to

Be more concerned with your character than your reputation, because character is what you really are, while your reputation is merely what others think you are.
                    — John Wooden, college basketball coach

I care not what others think of what I do, but I care very much about what I think of what I do. That is character.
                    — Theodore Roosevelt,
            twenty-sixth President of the United States

valid self-esteem. Winners never make room for negative thinking (not any champion *I've* ever met, and I know many). They know that they have only themselves to work with. If they're going to win, they have to discover their true interests, talents, and feelings and get it right—the positive things that will automatically work for them—not the negative things that work against them. Winning is programmed on the positive, the truths about ourselves that will help us win, not the truths about ourselves that will help us lose.

Sure, we all have our shortcomings—and by recognizing them honestly we can learn to deal with them, even overcome them. But we all have our special superiorities, too, and it is on these that all champions focus, building upon them day after day. This is exactly what occurs when you give yourself permission to win. As I said, it's automatic. You will instinctively recognize the unique qualities within yourself that make a winning game plan possible. In so doing, you'll rediscover the special qualities that give you reason for high self-esteem.

One man who is familiar with every word in this book said to me, "*Giving yourself permission to win isn't just a great motivational philosophy. When you take into account everything it does for you, it's an absolute resurrection from the dead.*"

3

WHAT IS WINNING?

Most people want to win. Many want it so much they can taste it. They want to put their losing ways behind them and go forward as winners. They want a fresh new start. They want to overcome their problems, to achieve, to feel right about themselves, to know what they're made of. They want to be up when they should be down. They want to give their very best.

Winning is all of those things—and much more. It's helping people and looking for the best in them, forgiving others (*and* yourself); it is burying the past and all the losing attitudes that held you back from success; it is stepping into a brand new life and approaching everything in a positive, confident way. Winning is fulfilling your mission in life. (You <u>do</u> have a mission, you know. Richard Bach, the author of *Jonathan Livingston Seagull* and *Illusions,* put it best when he said, *"Here's a test to find out if your mission in life is through: if you're alive, it is not."*)

Winning is acknowledging one of life's greatest truths—a truth often voiced by W. Mitchell, a friend of mine from the National Speakers Association who overcame tremendous adversity: *"It doesn't matter what happens to you, just what you* do *with what happens to you!"* (Remember the cancer kids—they understand that truth perfectly!) Winners never allow a terrible situation to defeat them.

Mr. Mitchell knows this firsthand—he was burned over 65% of his body in a motorcycle accident in San Francisco. Four years later, the plane he was piloting crashed on take-off, leaving him paralyzed and in a wheelchair. *"Before I was paralyzed,"* he says, *"there were 10,000 things I could do; now there are 9,000. I can either dwell on the 1,000 I've lost or focus on the 9,000 I have left."* His book, *The Man Who Would Not Be Defeated,* is one of the most inspiring autobiographies I have ever read.

Yes, most people want to accomplish the things I've just talked about. They truly want to be winners.

They just don't know <u>how</u>. They don't understand what it takes. They're eager to win, but they're not ready for it. They look at everything and everybody for permission to get ahead, to change their lives and fulfill their dreams—for permission to be winners. But that's not how it's done. If you've read this far, you know how it's done:

You have to give <u>yourself</u> that permission. And you understand what that means: you have to <u>decide</u> you're a winner—not just <u>hope</u> to be a winner, not just <u>think</u> you can be a winner—but decide that you <u>are</u> a winner.

Remember, nobody is a nobody and everybody is a somebody! You were not born in vain. There is a purpose for you. Everything in nature works that way. In one way or another—even if you are severely depressed,

---

I realize that success is having the courage to meet failure without being defeated. I also recognize that although I cannot always control what happens to me, I can control how I respond to my wins and losses.

— Phil Niekro, Major League pitcher

broke, handicapped, or stricken with a deadly disease—
you have been given the means and the talent and the
spirit to overcome your adversities. You just have to
give yourself *permission* to do it.

"Permission" means "consent" or "authorization."
When I was a child, I asked my mother for permission
to go out and play. I asked my teacher for permission
to go to the bathroom. When I was in the Air Force, I
had to ask for permission to do almost anything. It wasn't
until years later that I discovered what I was lacking
in my life—giving myself permission to win. That's just
what I did when I suddenly decided I was a winner and
flushed Mrs. Lemon and my losing attitude out of my
system. That was my January 1st, and from that point
forward I started to win, making each day that followed
a new January 1st, rising up each morning knowing I
was a winner—and my unfinished mission in life is to
help coach you into doing the same thing and reaping
the same winning results.

Are you coachable? Of course you are! You want
to win, or you wouldn't be reading this book. I believe
you now know that you have to be willing to let go of
yesterday and all the negative attitudes that have held
you back from winning. I believe that you realize your
future starts today. I believe you'll act intelligently on
that knowledge and give yourself permission to win.

Why wouldn't you? Everything you have to lose
is worthless. Everything you have to gain is priceless.
So I believe you have decided to be a winner and to
act on it—no more "maybes" or "ifs" or "buts"—and
with that decision, you are a winner.

---

*I sought advice and cooperation from all those around
me — but not permission.*

— Muhammad Ali, professional boxer

And we're talking about *today.* Right now. No matter where you are in your life at this moment, no matter how big a loser you may have thought you were, it's all part of yesterday—it's finished! This is a new day, a new beginning. *You are a winner!* That's your new mindset; it's part of you from this moment forward. And it's not me telling you that. <u>You're</u> telling <u>yourself</u>! This day, you are giving yourself the very first of those many priceless gifts in your future—you are giving yourself *permission to win!*

And I guarantee it will be permanent. You will not go back to the old ways of thinking. Never! Not as long as you make every day January 1st!

Now, exactly how does permission to win operate? How is it put into practice? You understand it in theory, but what are the mechanics of it? How do you apply it in <u>your</u> world to help achieve success, recognition, security, happiness, and growth? Or perhaps you want friendship or more energy or better health. Exactly how does "permission to win" work in real life to help you accomplish your goals and reach the most prized possessions of all—the ability to overcome every setback and achieve and maintain inner peace?

Well, that's what the rest of this book is about. Chapter by chapter, we'll cover the real-life application of "permission to win" in what I call the "Circle of Life." For most of us, that circle is a balance wheel with ten spokes—family, financial, educational, attitude, physical fitness, spiritual fitness, charity, goals, professional, and leisure. When you apply "permission to win" to each of those ten spokes, devoting an equal amount of time and attention to each, keeping them in balance, you'll have an awesome Circle of Life—and you'll be closer to that inner peace.

But for now, let me give you a clear example of "permission to win" in action. Let's go back to that Notre Dame locker-room I mentioned in the *Introduction* ...

Lou Holtz, the head coach of the legendary football team at the University of Notre Dame, had asked me to help prepare his players for the 1990 Orange Bowl (a game played each year on January 1st). It was the night before the game and there I was, standing in front of a bunch of guys who had a <u>real</u> problem. The game was to be played against the University of Colorado at the Orange Bowl in Miami, *but the Notre Dame players seemed convinced that they couldn't win in Miami!* They'd won every game they played that year, except against Miami (at Miami)—<u>plus</u> they hadn't won in the Orange Bowl for the past ten years! They felt that they just couldn't do it, so they looked upon Miami and the Orange Bowl as a curse. They were completely psyched out.

The first thing I did was to challenge the players, telling them that <u>not</u> to decide to win the Orange Bowl <u>was</u> to decide. I told them that if they had decided not to win, then the decision was made, they wouldn't win, and I might as well go home.

Well, they hadn't really decided <u>not</u> to win ... but they didn't <u>know</u> they could. I told them it was the same thing, and they began to get the picture.

The next thing I did was to present the co-captains with an imaginary trophy—the Orange Bowl trophy. I explained to them that I was doing this because I didn't want anyone to steal it.

I said to them that if I told you someone had broken into the house of a friend of yours and stolen his television set and VCR, you'd feel sorry for him. But if I told you that someone had broken into <u>your</u> house and stolen <u>your</u> TV and VCR, you'd have a much stronger reaction. By the time the evening was over, they'd made the decision that the imaginary Orange Bowl trophy I'd presented to them was theirs—it belonged to them, they had it in their possession—and they had no intention of allowing Colorado to break into their house and steal it!

Now they were approaching the game in an entirely new way. The Orange Bowl was their house ... it was their trophy ... it was their victory! I explained to them that the dimensions of a football field were the same in South Bend as they were in Miami at the Orange Bowl. The big difference this time was that they were giving themselves *permission to win!*

The next day, just before game-time and with Coach Holtz's blessing, I had Tony Rice, the quarterback, run the team down the sidelines and across the end-zone shouting *"OUR HOUSE! OUR HOUSE! OUR HOUSE!"* Colorado was shocked and appeared a little intimidated. National television played it out for the world to see. It was exciting! You could see the determination in the eyes of the Notre Dame players—they had gotten the message ... they believed it ... this was their house and they had already won!

In the third quarter, we were in a little bit of trouble. An offensive guard ran over to me and shouted: *"Coach! Coach! You sure we're still gonna win?"*

"Man," I said, *"I promise you you're gonna win!"* He reached down and picked me up (no small accomplishment; I weighed about 290 pounds) and he gave me a big, fat kiss on the cheek!

The final score of that 1990 Orange Bowl game was Notre Dame 21, Colorado 6. When we got back to the locker-room the young men got down on their knees, the priest blessed them, and then they sang the "Fighting Irish" song. Coach Holtz spoke, telling the players how proud he was of them and sharing his conviction that they played for the greatest university on planet Earth, but that they should be respectful when talking about the game and Colorado. He said they should build up Colorado and talk positively about them.

A class act, Lou Holtz. It's been one of my greatest privileges to count him among my friends, and the game ball he gave me that day—for giving his team permission to win the Orange Bowl—is among my most valued treasures.

Now, that's just one example of putting *permission to win* into action—of using it to overcome a losing attitude and scoring a victory when victory seems impossible. And while that should be the end of the Notre Dame story, it can't really be finished without adding the following footnote:

Life can be very strange at times. A few days before being invited to address the Notre Dame team, I had been asked to speak to the University of Miami Hurricanes before they left to play Alabama in the Sugar Bowl. Now get this: if the Hurricanes won that game, they would be the national champions—if Notre Dame beat Colorado in the Orange Bowl!

Of course, I didn't know I was going to be invited to help prepare the Notre Dame players for the Orange Bowl; the only appointment I had at the time was with the Hurricanes, and that was about the Sugar Bowl. So I went into the Hurricanes' locker room, talked with the

---

The whole idea is to somehow get an edge. Sometimes it takes just a little extra something to get that edge, but you have to have it.

— Don Shula, former NFL coach

coaches and players, got a feel for their attitude, and then focused on a theme I've used with dozens of championship teams. It essentially consists of one main question: I look into their eyes and ask, *"Why do you deserve to win?"*

They gave me the answers you'd expect:
"Because we're better coached."
"We have a better game plan."
"We're better conditioned."
"We've worked harder."
"We have a better strategy."

But there's a problem with those answers: they miss the point. The <u>other</u> team could give the same answers. So what's the difference that enables one team to win?

The difference, as I tell them, is <u>deciding!</u> The other team isn't their opponent. <u>They</u> are their opponent. They must <u>decide</u> to win! This is what gives them the winner's edge.

They made that decision in the locker room that day. I could hear it in their words, see it in their eyes, and read it in their souls. <u>Now</u> they were ready!

And they went on to win the Sugar Bowl.

With Notre Dame's win over Colorado, of course, the Hurricanes became the national champions that year.

There are many people who could be Olympic champions. All-Americans who have never tried. I'd estimate more than five million people could have beaten me in the pole vault the years I won it...at least five million. Men that were stronger, bigger, and faster than I was could have done it, but they never picked up a pole, never made the feeble effort to pick their legs off the ground trying to get over the bar.

— Bob Richards,
pole vaulter; two-time Olympic Gold Medalist

Both Notre Dame and the Hurricanes had given themselves *permission to win!* And I was thrilled to play a double role in those victories.

Two teams. Two winners. Two stories. I could tell you many more—in fact, I have five championship rings from Miami Senior High. Miami High's coach, Marcos "Shakey" Rodriguez (now head coach at Florida International University), gave me the privilege of working with the team to win five state championships in seven years. I'm grateful to him, as I am to the many coaches who have invited me to speak in team locker rooms at the professional, college, and high-school levels. Here are coaches and players who understand the first verse in what I call my Champion's Gospel: *As soon as losing is out of your mind, winning is in your hand!*

But the important thing is that <u>you</u> understand it! So now—from here on out—we're going to talk about putting *permission to win* to work in <u>your</u> life.

It will be exciting. Stay with me. You *are* a winner! *Decide*!

CIRCLE OF LIFE

The spokes in this wheel represent the essential components of life. Notice that each spoke of the wheel is numbered 0 to 10, with zero being the closest point to the center. Evaluate the time and attention you devote to each spoke (on a scale of 0 to 10) and mark the spokes accordingly. Then 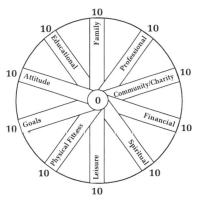 connect the marks. If your life is in perfect balance, you'll end up with a perfect circle. If you see bumps, you know the areas you need to work on.

You come closest to a life of fulfillment when there is balance in all the areas shown. The way you achieve that balance is by applying *permission to win* in the areas that clearly demand it.

From my research, the illustration to the right represents the <u>imbalance</u> found in the average life. *You can do better than this!* Decide! Give yourself *permission to win!* Bring your circle into balance and roll smoothly toward a life of fulfillment!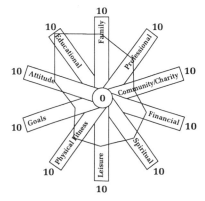

4

GOALS AND MISSIONS

What is your goal? Is it to own a home? Make a lot of money? Is it recognition and status? Fame and fortune? Do you want your own business?

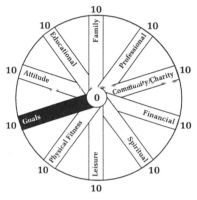

Most of us have several goals, but it's important to choose them with great care—because none of them will bring you lasting satisfaction unless they help you fulfill your mission in life. In fact, when you know what your mission is, you may find that the goals you've been pursuing in the past are exactly the wrong goals.

Your "mission" refers to your reason for being on earth, the purpose of your life. It is based on the vision you have of your place in the world and the difference you can make in the lives of others and on the planet.

All of us need a vision and a mission. In most cases, it's natural and instinctive—a combination of our talents, desires, and interests. It's who we really are. Sometimes it eats away at us. It tells us what we should be doing with our lives. And no matter how well we disguise it, it often shows through. People might say of others who seem to be in the wrong job that "*She was born to be a teacher,"* or *"He should have been a car-penter."* Maybe they see the truth.

Do you see the truth in yourself? Have you ever taken the time to just stop and explore your truth? Are you devoting your life to a career that doesn't bring you deep inner satisfaction and pride, that doesn't make the most of your talents? Are you denying yourself the ful-fillment of doing what you were meant to do? Are you sabotaging your mission?

Deep down, you should <u>know</u> what you were born to do; you should know your natural gifts and the things that interest you the most. It's something you should feel, something you may often think about and dream you were doing.

So, why aren't you doing it? What's holding you back? Is it your education? Your race? Is it money or the circumstances of your life? Dr. Martin Luther King, Jr. envisioned his mission and he invested his life in attempting to achieve it. *"I have a dream,"* he said, *"that my four small children will grow up in a country where they will be judged by the content of their character and not the color of their skin."*

Think of the goals Doctor King had to reach in his attempt to fulfill his mission! He had to rise from poverty. He had to learn to speak in public, make him-self heard, gather a following, organize his campaigns, become a leader. Imagine fulfilling all those goals and becoming the foremost spokesman for his people in his generation! He was a winner because he didn't compro-mise on what he knew was his lifetime mission—and he set the right goals to fulfill it as best he could. He paid a tremendous price. It cost him his life! He wasn't oblivious to the possibility of dying for his cause—he'd been threatened many times and spoke of the danger.

But he had a mission to fulfill and believed that even if he were martyred it was worth it to continue his work.

Most people with a mission are in no such danger—their mission is an adventure toward fulfillment and happiness. But it has to be the right mission. I'll bet some of the unhappiest people you know are those who have never set goals for themselves, or, more likely, they've set goals that have nothing to do with who they really are and their mission in life. They hate their jobs. They're doing everything they don't want to do. They're investing their lives in the wrong goals. They may be successful in fulfilling their goals, but they're cheating themselves when it comes to personal satisfaction and inner peace—the greatest goals of all.

It's amazing how many of these people I meet every day—people who feel like slaves. I don't care how successful they are or how prestigious their company may be or what their title is. They may be successful in the eyes of the world, but they never took the time to look into themselves and discover their true mission and the goals that would help them achieve it and bring them real fulfillment and happiness.

But this is not the way it will be for you. Remember, this is your January 1st—a new beginning for you. The past is gone, and that includes the old goals that weren't right for you, that weren't helping you fulfill your life's mission. So you can see that before you can decide on your goals, you have to recognize and define

---

By your own soul learn to live, and if men thwart you take no heed. If men hate you, have no care. Sing your song, dream your dream, hope your hope and pray your prayer.
— Verse admired by Adolph Rupp,
college basketball coach.
Author unknown.

your mission. This comes first—and when you define your mission, it is the most important time in your life to heed the ancient maxim: *"To thine own self be true."*

How do you do that? Well, my own mission is to have a positive effect on every human life I touch. I recognize that God has given me the talent to coach people into being the winners they're born to be, so to achieve my mission I have to establish specific goals in learning, communication, financial means, professional standards, and so on. Fulfilling these goals enables me to use my talent and go forward with my mission. To touch life positively.

Your mission—your deepest instinctive interest in life—might be to comfort or heal the sick. Suppose you find that this is the thing you want most to do. In that case, you may need to set educational and other goals that will help you become a nurse or doctor or medical technician ... or a hospice worker, a driver for Meals on Wheels, or a part-time companion for elderly shut-ins. Whatever the case, there are certain goals that you must first achieve—learning about hospice work, for example, or arranging your life to make time for driving and house visits.

I have a friend whose daughter feels compelled to help the very poorest of the Indian tribes in the Southwest. She was raised in the east, but aiding the Indians was her vision from childhood. She couldn't get away from it and knew it had to be her mission. Her first goal was to move west. Her second goal was to learn everything she could about the Indians' needs. Her third goal was to establish a food-distribution operation. She is a very fulfilled young woman. She has no money, no big house, no fancy car ... but she is achieving her mission, and the light dances in her eyes. She set the right goals to achieve her mission. She is true to herself.

Do you feel your mission is to help the environment—but your talents are in business? Then set your goals. Start a business, or join one, that helps the environment. You'll be good at it, and you'll be fulfilling your mission. You'll have more peace than the richest entrepreneur who, in his heart, knows that he should be helping his fellow man and the planet, but has elected to make millions doing the opposite.

It doesn't matter who you are or what you do— whether you're the CEO of a huge corporation or the person who mops the floors and empties the wastebaskets—you have the power to find the vision in your heart. You have been given a mission to fulfill that's as worthy as anyone's, whether it's to discover the cure for cancer or to manage a soup kitchen for the homeless or to chuck a high-paying job you hate and be the best plumber in East Nowhere, Alaska. Whatever it is, it's what your uniqueness and spirit and talents cry out for you to do, and you must recognize and define your mission before you set even one goal for the future.

So do it now. Inspect yourself. Give yourself the most thorough gut-check of your life. Think about it

---

Although they only give gold medals in the field of athletics, I encourage everyone to look into themselves and find their own personal dream, whatever that may be — sports, medicine, law, business, music, writing, whatever. The same principles apply. Turn your dream into a goal and learn how to attack that goal systematically. Break it into bite-size chunks that seem possible, and then don't give up. Just keep plugging away.

— John Naber, swimmer; four-time Olympic Gold Medalist

big-time. Struggle to really know yourself. Keep your long-range happiness and fulfillment in mind. If you knew you were going to die today, how would you feel about yourself? Was your life productive and worth-while? Were you true to yourself? Was it right? Did you achieve your mission? Did you do what you know you were meant to?

If the answer doesn't please you, then *change your goals*. This is your January 1st. Change starts today! This is the day you set the right goals. This is the day you give yourself permission to accomplish your mission!

Finally, it's very important for you to put your mission into words—a mission statement. You can do it. And once you do, write it down. Unless it's written, it's just a wish. Writing it down makes it concrete and specific. It keeps you focused.

Don't worry about whether your mission is real-istic or not. It will automatically be realistic. If you're seventy years old, for example, and always wanted to be an airline pilot, you know it's not going to happen and it will no longer be your mission. You'll instinc-tively have a different mission in mind. Everyone's instinctive mission reflects the possible. Instinct is the real you talking, including your common sense that tells you what you can do and what you can't do. Instinct sets your mission, and it will reveal not only what you want to do and should do, but also what you can do if you focus on it with a winning attitude and set the right goals to achieve it.

So now's the time to determine your mission in life and put your **mission statement** on paper. Writing it down makes it real. My own personal mission state-ment—*to have a positive effect on every human life I touch*—is not only written down, I've included it in published articles. My company's mission statement, which further defines and expands my own, is framed and hanging on the office wall:

> The Pelletier Group is a unique Global Communications Team dedicated to coaching and inspiring companies and individuals to develop positive beliefs, understanding, and a compelling vision ... until no one is left under the bleachers.

(The reference to "bleachers" is there to remind me of the teenage girl who hid herself under the bleachers after I'd spoken in a high school gymnasium. She'd hidden there so she could talk with me privately about a serious personal problem after the other students had left. I'd almost missed seeing her on my way out ... but I did see her, thank God, and I was able to offer the help she needed. Actively seeking out people who need help—making sure to the best of our ability that no one is left "under the bleachers"—best expresses my company's deepest concern and is an essential part of our mission statement.)

A mission statement doesn't have to be profound or flowery, or long or short—it just has to reflect who you really are and the work in life you <u>know</u> in your soul you'd love to do and were born to do. The plainer you can make it, the better.

This past summer, a friend of mine saw the following mission statement written out in pencil on a card and displayed on the dashboard of his handyman's truck:

> Think trees ... trees ... trees.

Two months later, the handyman quit coming to my friend's house—he had landed a full-time job with the county's Woods Conservation Commission. He was on the way to fulfilling his mission!

When you've decided on your own mission statement and set it out in writing, you'll be ready to define the goals that will help you achieve your dream. So I ask you again to put this book down and really think about your mission statement and write it out.

I believe some of you will do that right now. And I hope all of you will do it. Because as soon as you've defined your life's mission and written it down, it means the dress rehearsal is over—now you can start doing what it takes to achieve your dream and meaningful fulfillment. Once you've written your mission statement down, it's the real thing. There's no more waiting.

It's game time!

I'm glad you now know your mission in life. But I can't crawl into your head and see what it is. All I know is that whatever your mission may be—and whatever specific goals must be met to achieve it—certain fundamental rules apply.

First, have no doubt that you will attain your goals and complete your mission. You are giving yourself *permission to win!* It's done. There's no debate. *Decide!* Not to decide is to decide!

Second, visualize your game plan. Know exactly what you want to accomplish, the specific goals you must achieve to get there, and the way the game will turn out. Play the whole scenario in your head from start to finish. Prior to every speaking engagement, I mentally rehearse the entire program. Before I step onto the platform, I know what I'm going to do and what it will take to accomplish my purpose.

Jack Nicklaus, the famous golfer, says that golf is 50% skill and 50% mental. The night before a game, he mentally plays it out, hole by hole, putting himself in the winner's circle at the end of the game. He is a champion. He knows you have to <u>live</u> your game and experience it in your mind before you can attain victory. By visualizing his entire game plan, Nicklaus can adjust his strategies to improve his chances at every hole. He's not stuck in the past. Old strategies might not work. He can adjust his play to the expected weather, the condition of the greens, and to everything else that might affect his game. All consistent champions visualize their challenges before they face them   ... in sports, in business, in life.

It's important for you to do the same thing. Whatever your game plan, play it all out in your mind. Strategize. Take everything into account. Recognize the goals you must attain to be successful. Be innovative. And don't be afraid to change your strategy when circumstances change. Keep your eye on the winning objective: *doing what you are meant to do in life.* Be relentless about it!

Do that, and your innate intelligence will show you exactly what your goals should be and how to achieve them. But there's one thing more: you must be committed and passionate. You must make your dream <u>live</u> in your mind!

When I was a youngster, one of things that kept me going was the encouragement I got from Walt Disney each Sunday evening, and especially from the words in a song from one of the wonderful Disney movies: *"When you wish upon a star ... "*

I want you to do that.

That's right: I want you to wish upon a star. I want you to think like an adult, but <u>dream</u> like a kid again. Your potential is unlimited. You can accomplish anything you believe you can accomplish! You need those wonderful dreams as much as you need grown-up common sense and determination and energy. You need the spirit and passion and heart and optimism you had when you were young enough to <u>know</u> that everything was possible. Because it really is! Everything you hope to be is all out there waiting for you. Dream about it as if you were a kid. But figure it all out as an adult— every challenge, every goal that has to be achieved, every step that leads to success. Then go for it like a high-school fullback! Remember, this is your January 1st. You're starting all over again.

Don't forget the kid part!

Third, be patient. Overnight success takes time. Often in my seminars I remind people of that fact with this little vignette: I looked into the face of God and said, *"God, how much is a million dollars to you?"* And he looked back at me and said, *"A penny."* I said, *"God, how long is a million years to you?"* And he said, *"A minute."* And then I said, *"Please, God, may I have just a penny?"* And he looked back at me and said, *"In just a minute."*

Patience is a goal in itself—one of the most important ones. Remember that. Work on it. Don't be frustrated. Don't be discouraged. If you've been honest with yourself about who you are and your mission in life, then you'll make better goal choices than you've ever made before. In a word, you'll work <u>smarter</u> ... and your patience will pay off.

Never tell a young person that something cannot be done. God may have been waiting for centuries for somebody ignorant enough of the impossible to do that thing.

— Dr. J.A. Holmes, American clergyman

What does "working smarter" mean? I'm sure you've heard the phrase, *"It's not working harder that counts, it's working smarter."* That simple phrase embodies the prerequisites for success.

Working smarter means that you need to set goals. You need to understand yourself, to communicate better, to collaborate. You need to build your education. You need to serve others, and you need the right tools to do it. In this chapter, let's take the word "smarter," break it down into its letters, and apply it to building SMARTER goals.

The "S" in "smarter" stands for <u>specific</u>. You've already been specific about your mission. Now you must be just as specific about each of the goals you need to reach to fulfill your mission. Think of each goal as a branch on a tree. Your mission is to reach the top of the tree. Once you've climbed that tree in your mind (visualizing your game plan), you'll know the branches you'll have to grab to reach the top. It will be very clear to you. Some branches will help you get to the top. Some won't. If you don't choose them very specifically beforehand, you'll fall to the ground. Goals are like those branches—they must be specific.

The "M" in "smarter" stands for <u>measurable</u>. Being patient about obtaining your goals is one thing. Not being able to measure your progress is something else. You need a mental lift when things are going slowly, and one of the good things about having specific goals is that your progress in reaching them is always measurable. If one of your necessary goals, for example, is earning a nursing degree, then at least you'll know you're getting there when you've signed up for classes or passed

your first exams. You'll feel good about yourself ...
you'll know you're focused ... you'll know you're
starting to climb the tree.

Contrast that with a person who doesn't recognize his or her mission and has no set goals other than
to go to work each day, do an uninteresting job, and
then come home and get ready to do the same thing all
over again the next day. This isn't happening to you.
Each day—when you work at specific goals—you'll see
measurable movement toward the life you were meant
to live.

The "A" stands for <u>attainable</u>. Your goals must be
attainable. Well, that's not a problem for you. You already know you have the right goals, and because you've
given yourself *permission to win* you know in your heart
that you'll attain your goals and fulfill your mission.

You see, that's what *permission to win* is all about.
Your dream is attainable only if you allow it to be. It's
a mental decision. That's why I believe that the following ten two-letter words are among the most important
in the English language: *"If it is to be, it is up to me."*
When you believe those words, you are immediately
free to attain your goals. Only <u>you</u> can hold yourself
back. But you won't do that. You'll find a way. You
have the right stuff. You <u>know</u> it. And because you know
it, you'll attain your goals!

The "R" stands for <u>realistic</u>. As I said before, if
your mission is based on your instinctive awareness of
who you really are and the calling you were born to
follow, then it is automatically realistic. When your goals
are based on that dream, they also will tend to be
realistic.

Now, while your goals will be realistic for your purposes, they might not always seem realistic to others. But so what? It's your dream, not theirs! You'll probably have to break some rules to get to your objective. You're not going to allow money, time, and pressures to restrict you in the pursuit of your mission. You'll work around these problems. You'll be innovative and determined. You won't give up! And I promise you, you'll have a good time doing it!

But you have to be wary of what is not realistic. It can be tricky. If your mission is based not on your instincts, but on a passing fancy, then your goals will not be realistic and you will probably fail—no matter how dedicated you might be. Never forget that you have to be true to your deepest instincts, values, and talents. Go back to your mission statement and focus on it. Be sure it reflects the real you before you define your goals to achieve your dream. If you're 100% realistic about your mission, everything that follows should also be realistic.

The "T" stands for timely. Anything you can do to aid the human race and the planet is timely. But sometimes that may involve the designing or selling of a helpful new product or service, and it's important to know that there's a ready market for it. Look around, use your common sense, do some research, and set your goals accordingly. This is where being realistic really pays off.

For example, suppose your mission is to help the environment and one of your goals is to start a home business selling ecologically safe household cleaning products. That's a very worthy cause. Everyone knows they should use such products, but they don't. So, the market's there—your business goal is timely—but you have to figure out a good way to call attention to your products. How do you do that? Well, I could talk about innovative promotion ideas and hope that they fit your particular goal, but that's not the real key. That's not where success starts. That's not what this book is about. The real key is to <u>decide</u> right now that you <u>will</u> find the right solution to every challenge you'll face.

Believe me, with that attitude you <u>will</u> find those solutions. You can count on it!

The "E" stands for <u>exciting</u>! Here's where your passion and commitment come in—that wonderful and necessary "kid" attitude I talked about earlier. Each goal you complete is a branch up the tree to the completion of your mission and your dream. Be excited about it! You're getting there! It's worth it! You'll win! You can't spend time on yesterday and all the negative attitudes that held you back. Hey, *you can't smell yesterday's roses!* This is a new day for you. This is the day you start to really be yourself—the greatest gift you've ever received. Be <u>excited!</u>

And, finally, the last "R" in "smarter" stands for <u>ready</u>, get set, and go! Just do it! Decide! No holding off. No more excuses. You're allowed a five-minute pity party for all your past mistakes. No more. That's it. Today, you're giving yourself *permission to win.* Today, you are <u>ready</u>!

SMARTER goals—you'll need them every step of the way to succeed in the years ahead.

The world is moving so fast these days that the man who says it can't be done is generally interrupted by someone doing it.

— Elbert Hubbard, American editor/writer

5

ATTITUDE—THE MAGIC OF MENTAL COACHING

Right now, this is what I believe about you.

I believe you have <u>truly</u> given yourself *permission to win.* You understand the concept. You recognize its tremendous potential for you. You're just starting to try it on, but already there's a new excitement in your thinking. You're beginning to think as 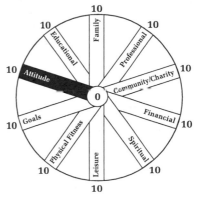 a winner—and you <u>like</u> it! You're not used to it, but it's great to realize you can approach life with the winner's attitude you were meant to have. Even now, at this early stage, you sense the profound effect it can have on your life.

But that is only the beginning.

I believe that as you grow in your understanding of how *permission to win* operates, it will naturally become your <u>primary</u> form of thinking ... even instinctive. You'll automatically apply your winning attitude to the countless varieties of challenges that face you in every area of your life—family, career, health ... all the spokes of the wheel in the Circle of Life. It will just happen naturally. You'll deal with every challenge from your winner's viewpoint.

So get ready for a <u>big</u> change in your thinking!

But, as every champion knows, there is a price to pay in maintaining a winner's edge. It's not a free ride.

Will you pay the price? That's the million-dollar question. Will you consistently do what you have to do to make your winner's attitude work for you? I believe that you will.

To maintain your winning attitude, you have to develop a set of disciplines. Remember, you're only a winner as long as you <u>know</u> you're a winner, and there are certain things you'll need to do every day to <u>keep</u> knowing it! There are certain ways you'll have to train. Certain influences you'll need to cultivate. Certain surroundings in which you should place yourself. Certain assurances and motivations that should always be present. In short, to maintain your winning attitude and keep it in championship form, what you need is a real <u>coach</u>—a coach who unquestionably has your best interests at heart.

The right coach will keep you confident that you're a winner and never let you delude yourself into thinking otherwise. The right coach will never let you get so down on yourself that you start thinking losing thoughts. The right coach will give you a daily attitude check and see that you come up with the right one. The right coach will see to it that everything you do in life will be a positive influence and help you think and act like the winner you are.

What it takes to be number one: You've got to pay the price. Winning is not a sometime thing; it's an all-the-time thing. You don't win once in a while; you don't do things right once in a while; you do them right all the time. Winning is a habit. Unfortunately, so is losing.

— Vince Lombardi, NFL coach

Today, you're allowing me to be that coach. But when you're done with this book, then what? Where will you find a coach who will keep you in training and see to it that you stay solidly in the winner's circle for the rest of your life?

Where will you find a coach like that?

Look in the mirror. There's your coach.

There's no way I'll coach you into giving yourself *permission to win* and then walk off the field without showing you how to protect and strengthen that winning attitude for as long as you live. Before this chapter is finished, you'll begin to understand how to mentally coach <u>yourself</u> during all the years to come.

How do you coach yourself mentally?

First of all, let's have a look at something each of us has: <u>two</u> minds.

As you probably know, each of us has a conscious mind and a subconscious mind. The conscious mind is aware of the things around us and the things that happen to us. The decisions we make, the information we take in, the tapes and music we hear, the books we read, the TV programs we watch—all of these things are impressed upon our conscious mind.

Our subconscious mind, on the other hand, is where we have our memory bank. Everything our conscious mind decides to remember is stored in our subconscious mind. As a consequence, the subconscious mind is what really programs us.

For example, if I remember being told I was a loser by Mrs. Lemon, I might not be consciously aware of it every minute, but it's tucked away in my subconsciousness. The moment I dare to think that I might really be a winner, Mrs. Lemon's negative programming comes to the surface and affects me. It makes me think twice. It holds me back from making a decision. Maybe she was right. Maybe I'm really *not* a winner.

The subconscious mind, then, is an extremely powerful motivator. It can be your best friend ... or your worst enemy! It depends on what's in it—negative stuff or positive stuff. Whichever it is—whichever sub-conscious programming is the most memorable and most powerful—it will tend to dominate your thoughts and feelings and views about yourself and your life. It is totally controlling, *and if you're going to be a long-term winner, you have to access your subconscious mind and reprogram it with the positive thoughts and experiences that will keep you on top!*

I remind you again that you have given yourself *permission to win.* This is your January 1st. Yesterday is gone. You're erasing every negative tape that you can find in your subconscious storage bin. From now on, to keep your winning attitude, you have to be extremely selective about the new tapes you put into that storage bin. You have to be careful about what you expose your mind to! From this day forward, you need to expose your subconscious mind to positive influences that will strengthen and preserve your winner's edge.

For two years, I took part in an in-house televi-sion program (Inmate Correctional TV) for about 2,000 inmates at the Dade County Jail in Florida. The severity of negative experiences and thoughts instilled in some of these men from the time they were children is im-possible to imagine. Even hearing it, you wouldn't believe it! The horror programming these men were exposed to makes Mrs. Lemon look saintly.

Most of these prisoners had a self-esteem level of Absolute Zero. Their whole subconscious package was negative. Every thought most of them had about themselves added up to "big-time loser." I gave myself the job of convincing them that they weren't—maybe the most demanding coaching work I've ever done—and here and there I think it was successful. But *man!*

There's an old phrase: *"Garbage in; garbage out."* Never was a truer phrase written. You <u>are</u> what your subconscious is, and when your subconscious is negative, so are you.

Dr. Maxwell Maltz, a world-famous plastic surgeon, wrote a book entitled *Psycho-Cybernetics*—a good book, easy to read and very informative. His report on the results of his surgeries is fascinating. Some of his patients were unhappy with the results; they didn't think they looked as good as they'd hoped they would. Other patients were delighted with the surgery. He worked up psychological profiles on both groups and discovered that those with a positive self-image of themselves prior to the surgery were <u>invariably</u> pleased with the results. But those with poor self-esteem before surgery—a poor self-image of themselves—were invariably <u>dis</u>pleased with the results.

The contrast was striking—and it tells us something. It tells us that negative input equals negative output (garbage in; garbage out). As sure as night follows day, you can't be a consistent winner if you're dominated by negative subconscious programming. It won't happen. Believe it!

So, what kind of plan can we come up with to help you reprogram your subconscious mind? Now that

---

Negative thoughts are contagious and they get passed around like a disease. I try to inoculate myself from the fear of failure.

— Bill Foster, college basketball coach

you've given yourself *permission to win* and erased the negative tapes of the past, what can you do to replace those tapes with positive images that will help you strengthen and maintain your winning attitude?

One thing that works for me is to start each day by repeating to myself that *I am not what I was, and I'm not what I'm going to be. But today I am working harder to become a better me.* It's just a couple of sentences, but it gets me properly focused when I stumble out of bed. It's a positive start. It means I'm not going to beat myself up over yesterday. Today is a new day. I will encourage myself, motivate myself, challenge myself. It means that today I will take time to focus on my goals and my mission and I will do at least one positive thing to further them. Today will be a winning day. Today, I will make progress toward my dream. Repeat those words to yourself every morning and you can't help but start the day with a winner's attitude. It works for me.

The next thing I try to do each morning is read something positive. This book is positive reading. So are many other books. Poetry. Inspirational verses. And certainly the Bible. Books that have a bearing on your mission, that give you information about it and how to prepare yourself, are very positive. Positive reading is a major success tool for champions, and I want to make use of that tool first thing in the morning to help me invest wisely in the day ahead.

Another thing I try to do each morning is take a walk and listen to a motivational tape while I'm at it. When I finish one side of the tape, I turn around and head home, listening to the other side. Not all of us can spare the time in the morning to walk or jog, but we all know we need exercise and should find time for some kind of early morning workout. Try to fit it in. Exercising both your mind and body first thing in the morning makes you feel like a winner. There's something about it. It works. Make reading and exercise the first of your positive influences for the day. There's no better way to get off to a winning start.

If positivism is your biggest friend, then negativism is your biggest enemy. Let's talk about negativism for a moment. You don't want it in your mind. You don't want it in your house. You don't want it in your environment. You don't want negativism in your friends and associates. You don't want anything to do with it.

Recently, I decided to donate blood, but I confess I was hesitant about it. I was concerned about AIDS. I was afraid I might get it from the health-care worker ... did she have gloves on? Was she using a new needle? Did the room look clean? Did everybody know what they were doing? But there's something I fear even more than catching AIDS. I fear negative thinking. My chances of contracting AIDS in that clinic were millions to one. But by not giving blood, my chances of contracting negativism were 100%. That was a guaranteed killer. I couldn't allow it.

My mind is winner-programmed. It is programmed to make me all that I can be. My limitations have been taken away. I dream my dreams and know that I'm achieving them. Everything about me and the way I think is based on being positive. I want nothing to do with negativism. I don't want to be around people who have fearful mindsets. I certainly won't tolerate it in myself. The one fear I do have—the only one—is of negativism. Wherever I find it, I run away from it as fast as I can. It scares me to death.

I have two sisters-in-law of whom I am very proud—Joan and Mary. After they were forty years old, both of them decided they wanted to be nurses. They inspected their deepest feelings and instincts and knew they wanted to be of service to the community, and that their talents, instincts, and interests pointed them toward nursing. They went through the entire educational process, accomplished all of their learning goals, got their nursing degrees, and then went out into the community to fulfill their mission of touching lives in a very positive way.

Both sisters had children—Joan, in fact, has nine children—but they believed they could achieve their dream, and they did. I tell you, during the long days and nights of study, these middle-aged women were as upbeat and as positive and confident as any kid dreaming of someday walking on the moon. Negativism? Not in those households! Did they think they were too old to study and become nurses? No way! Was there too little money? Too little time? Were there too many other demanding commitments? Would their contemporaries think they were foolish? They confronted every one of these fears and overcame them. They saw themselves only at their best. They knew what they could do and what they could be. They had a dream and they went for it—it was as if they had blinders on, seeing only the positive prize at the end of the tunnel. And they <u>won</u>!

As a result, both Mary and Joan are fulfilled, independent, and happy. Hundreds of people—their patients—are pleased that they went for their dream. The

---

I never think about my age. I let other people worry about it. Age is a state of mind. You can be old at 30 if you don't have enthusiasm and you can be young at 45 if you do.
— Pete Rose, former Major League first baseman/manager

two women are great nurses and they're making a positive difference.

Napoleon Hill is an author to whom I'll be grateful for the rest of my life. One of his books is called *Think and Grow Rich*. Andrew Carnegie, the American industrialist and humanitarian, commissioned Hill to study 157 of the most successful men and women in the world. He studied the old greats, such as Ford and Edison and the Rockefellers, and he interviewed them for hundreds of hours to find out just what it was they had that made them so special.

Do you know what it boiled down to? It was this: *they knew they could do it. Without exception, every one of them had a positive self-image and an undying belief that they could accomplish what they set out to do.*

If you think you can, you can. If you think you can't, you can't. Either way, you're right. The absolute power of the mind is staggering! You must do everything you can to program your subconscious mind with positive influences.

How can you give yourself positive influences? Where do you find them? What does it take?

First, you have to look at yourself. Are you a positive influence on yourself? You've already given yourself *permission to win*, so you know you're a winner. You've erased the negative tapes and self-images of the past—you've made a great start! Right now, you are a positive influence on yourself.

Now let's look at the rest of it. Let's start with the people you associate with.

For the past several years, when I'm not on the road, I've enjoyed the privilege of having breakfast at a local Miami restaurant. It's not fancy at all. It's a lot like the old TV sitcom "Cheers"—a place where "every-body knows your name."

We're an interesting collection of people at break-fast. We have mechanics, CEOs, CPAs, customer service reps, a bug exterminator, and a coach or two—among many others.

You wouldn't think we'd have too much in com-mon, but we do. It's an amazingly loose, upbeat, <u>positive</u> bunch—they seem to have collected at this place, and out of it has come an unspoken fraternity of sorts. While we don't talk about business—and while we can be merciless in seeing to it that nobody gets away with anything—there's an understanding that we believe in each other as human beings. <u>Really</u> believe. It's in the air, in our back-and-forth small-talk. We're positive about each other; we encourage each other. Title, money, physical appearance, nationality, race, religion—none of that matters. What matters is that we care about each other. We're <u>good</u> for each other.

There are places like that. Places where positive, supportive people come together. This little restaurant is one of them ... and these people have enriched my life. They're the right people to associate with.

Ask yourself—are the people you associate with negative or positive? How do they influence you? Are their priorities the same as yours? Do they have a mission in life? Are they of like mind with you? Do they believe in what you're doing? Are they upbeat, confident, with a never-say-die attitude? Are they givers? Do you get the feeling when you're around them that they're winners? Are you comfortable in their company? Do their words and ideas stimulate and reinforce your own objectives?

If your answers are "no," then their influence on you is negative and you need to change the company you keep. Winners need the company of winners. Winners learn from winners. When you associate with losers, their attitudes can subtly rub off. You don't need their input—it's the very last thing you need to maintain your winning attitude. Avoid them.

Is your <u>environment</u> a positive influence? Are you surrounded with winning images and tools—or is it just the opposite? In my home, I surround myself with things that reflect success, things that remind me of winning and where I want to be, things that keep me focused on my mission. I <u>want</u> true victory. I want to see it represented wherever I look. Like a champion who stands in the middle of a baseball diamond or football field on his day off, I need to <u>visualize</u> victory and <u>feel</u> it and <u>live</u> it in my mind. I need to <u>see</u> it around me. That way, I know I'll get it.

I don't have time to contemplate things or to be in places that don't further my mission. I have to be intimately involved with my dream, and so does everything in my environment.

Winners <u>dress</u> like the champions they expect to be. By that, I mean that you should keep yourself well-groomed and neat, one of the evidences of well-being and success. Do you know that in a tenth of a second people form an opinion about you just by the way you look? It's true, and you want to be sure people look at you and give you a winner's respect. In the beginning, there may be times when you haven't yet earned the respect due a champion—but it's important that others always <u>see</u> you as a champion. It will encourage you. It will bolster your self-image. By dressing like a winner, you'll be seen as a winner and you'll feel like a winner—a feeling that helps you overcome the obstacles you face. That's the positive atmosphere in which you need to operate. You don't necessarily need a new wardrobe. Just a new mindset.

The bottom line is that you always want to do everything you can to see to it that wherever you are, and under whatever circumstances, there is positive feedback—a positive atmosphere and environment—that influences you in the right way and builds your winner's image of yourself.

Next, do you <u>ask the pros</u>? This can be a tremendously positive influence in your life! They have the answers you're looking for. They know how it's done. No matter what your mission in life may be, someone has been there before you, and there's no better way to build up your winner's attitude and go on to victory than to seek out the experts in your field and listen to them.

In the National Speakers Association (I served on the National Board of Directors), we have hundreds of people with real-world experience as speakers. In order for new speakers to learn from them and gain as much expertise as possible in the shortest amount of time, we bring small groups through a "Meet the Pros" session. They sit at a table with a subject-matter expert and learn shortcuts to becoming the best speakers they can be.

The pros at these sessions are all positive, highly respected in their fields, and open to sharing the truths and the wisdom that will ease the way for novice speakers and help them to fulfill their missions. It's magic to watch the light of understanding take hold and to see the encouragement in the novices' eyes! In a matter of a few hours they can absorb a lifetime of others' hard-won knowledge and experience.

Get to know the pros in your field. Know where to find them. Seek them out. Associate with them as often as you can. *Don't be afraid to ask them for their knowledge.* I've always found that the best pros are the least hesitant to share. They're confident about themselves. They're happy to tell you what they know. They <u>want</u> to help you and guide you toward accomplishing your dream. They're not afraid to share, so *don't you be afraid to ask.* The speakers in our "Meet the Pros" sessions consider it an honor to instruct the novices. And boy! Can they ever help you along the way to being a winner!

Years ago, I proposed a major piece of business to the Burger King Corporation. In fact, it was bigger than anything I had ever dreamed of before. They informed me that although they'd like to give me the business, they were going to give it to Zig Ziglar in Dallas, Texas. I had tremendous respect for Zig. I had read his book, *See You At The Top*, and had listened to his self-help and sales tapes for years.

I was disappointed about losing the business. But even at that early stage in my career, I realized that every failure can be an opportunity—and here was a big one staring me in the face if I just had the guts to go for it. I obviously needed to learn more about selling myself to a major corporation. Maybe I could learn. So I turned to the two Burger King executives I was negotiating with and asked them for a big personal favor—would they please call Zig and ask him if I could sit in on the negotiations in Texas and see how he sells to one of America's largest companies?

They agreed. They called Zig, and he said, *"Come on!"*

A pessimist is one who makes difficulties of his opportunities; an optimist is one who makes opportunities of his difficulties.

— Harry Truman, thirty-third President of the United States

Wow! Zig was one of the truly top pros in the same marketplace I was involved in. I was a relative nobody. Yet he was willing to share his expertise and show me how big-league selling was done. This had to be one of the greatest growth opportunities of my life!

It was thrilling to see the master in action—by far the most instructive and fascinating hours I'd ever experienced in my budding career—and I believe that watching Zig Ziglar sell to Burger King *literally saved me five full years in the development of my business!*

Thank you, Zig Ziglar! And thank you, Burger King!

But remember, none of this would have happened if I hadn't <u>asked</u>.

So, ask the pros ... the ones with the quality and success you're striving for ... the experts who are where you want to be and whom you want to surpass. Listen to them. Watch them. Study them. Talk with them. Take it all in. Stay in their company as much as possible. Learn everything you can.

Then do your own thing in your own unique way—not duplicating what they do in every respect, but designing your own programs and methods that allow you to be <u>yourself</u> at your very best.

Understanding how you are programmed by your subconscious, thinking positive thoughts, surrounding yourself with positive people and a positive environment, avoiding negativism wherever you find it, associating with the pros in your field—these are the basic self-coaching disciplines that will help you reprogram your mind and realize your winner's potential. That's what good coaching is all about, and you're going to be that good coach.

There are many other disciplines we'll be touching on in coming chapters—the art of communication, listening and expressing yourself, value systems, spiritual and physical fitness, teamwork and collaboration, and much more.

None of it is complicated. It's mostly a matter of common sense. Remember, you're entrusted with keeping yourself the winner that you are. You are both the coach and the champion you're coaching. You have to take care of each other.

I believe that you'll do that. Nothing in this world will keep you from being the coach and the champion you are. You'll never go back to where you were yesterday. You have visualized the future and everything you're going to be. You won't let yourself down.

Why do I believe that? I believe it because <u>you</u> believe it! You have given yourself *permission to win*— and I know exactly how that operates. You will seek the champion in yourself. You will support that champion. There's no other way for you. No other way at all. You <u>are</u> a winner!

You put out, boy. You suck up your gut, give it all you've got and you give me that second effort. You give me that much, boy ... and I'll show you glory!

— Paul "Bear" Bryant,
college football coach and Athletic Director

6

LEARNING MAKES IT HAPPEN

You'd be surprised how many of today's most successful people were poor students in school. Some were even dropouts. They were convinced they couldn't learn ... couldn't do anything right ... didn't have any skills ... didn't fit into the learning scene. Put yourself in a roomful of today's

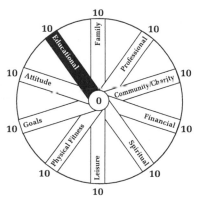

leaders in business, science, sports, or the arts and you'll hear that story over and over again.

But there's another story you'll hear from those same leaders: from the moment they first discovered their mission in life and knew who they really were and what they had to do, their whole attitude toward studying and learning was completely changed. All of a sudden, they were eager to obtain the information and knowledge that would help them grow and that would empower them to attain their dreams.

As one CEO put it when he finally recognized his mission, it was like falling in love for the first time: *"For years, you stumble around doubting you'll ever be in love. Then you meet someone—and whammo! Right away, you have a whole new set of priorities. Winning that someone is the only thought in your head and you do whatever it takes."*

Whammo time for you is right now—*and you know it!* Today's the day! All of a sudden, you've found a real love—your mission in life. You've even put it in writing. You now have a whole new set of exciting priorities! You know the goals you have to meet to win your dream. You know there are things you need to learn, skills to acquire, new information to collect. And, most important, you've given yourself the *permission* to go for it. To do whatever it takes. You're ready!

But are you ready? We need to make sure.

In my experience as a coach, I've learned that negative feelings about learning and education are the number-one hindrance people face in putting their *permission to win* into action and pursuing their dreams. Negative views toward learning usually come early in life and stick to us like a glove. In later life, when we need to update our skills or acquire new ones, we pull out those old tapes and start doubting our ability to learn new things. We're afraid we'll fail. If that's your situation, then it's my first responsibility as your coach to get you to destroy those negative tapes. I mean now— and no kidding!

I'll start by asking you two questions:

What does it matter if you have negative memories of school?

What does it matter if you were a poor student and had trouble retaining things, or if you hated studying and always doubted your learning abilities?

The honest, realistic, real-world answer to both questions is that it absolutely and positively doesn't matter at all! And I'll tell you why.

Those negative tapes are yesterday's tapes.

Yesterday, the time wasn't right for you.

Yesterday, the challenge wasn't right.

The motivation wasn't right.

The desire wasn't right.

The learning environment wasn't right.

<u>Nothing</u> was right!

Yesterday, you didn't know who you really were.

Yesterday, you didn't know what your mission was.

Yesterday, you didn't know you were a winner.

Yesterday, not one of those positive things existed for you ... not <u>one</u>! Yesterday, you weren't hungry to learn—you doubted you'd ever use the things you were studying!

<u>Today</u>, your situation is entirely different. Today, you're <u>motivated</u>—the most action-packed word in the English language. Those old negative tapes don't tell you anything about yourself <u>today</u>. They don't tell you anything about your ability to learn and grow <u>today</u>. They don't reflect your motivation and eagerness to get the knowledge and training you need to achieve your dreams. *You are not who you were yesterday!* This is a whole new ballgame. A whole new set of circumstances and enthusiasms and drives. A whole new <u>you</u>!

The only thing those old tapes do is provide life-support for the negative views and false limitations of the past. You're better than that! Get <u>rid</u> of that old stuff! <u>Now</u>!

I want you to remember a fundamental fact: *There's a huge difference between your God-given limitations and the limitations you create for yourself with negativity!*

For example, if you sensibly conclude that you will never be an Einstein because you have absolutely no interest in theoretical physics—no interest at all, no

instinct for it, no talent, no nothing—you're wisely recognizing a legitimate, inborn limitation in respect to
being a physicist. That's not negativity. That's common
sense.

On the other hand, if you instinctively love physics—have a talent for it, find it exciting and challenging,
and dream of making it your life's work—but decide not
to pursue it because some teacher told you in tenth grade
that you'd never achieve professional standards, then you're
creating a mental limitation for yourself. That's negativity.
It causes you to steal from yourself.

I could give you many other examples, but I'm
sure you get the point. Whatever you do, don't let
negative, December 31st thoughts of your past schooling
keep you from the education you need today to realize
your dream! Inspect your reasoning. Recognize the
difference between legitimate limitations and the limitations you create for yourself. Remember—and I repeat—
this is a different time with different circumstances.

Today is January 1st. Today you are motivated!
You're excited! You have a purpose. You are pursuing
your dream! You're a winner—a completely different
person—and the way you may have approached learning in the past will be light-years away from the enthusiasm and pleasure and sheer exuberance you will bring
to it now. You'll absorb every bit of learning that will
help you achieve your dream and not because you're
trying to get an "A." You're working to learn, grow, and
capture the knowledge you <u>know</u> you can use!

And I'll tell you this: I don't care if you were the
poorest and least interested student in every school you

---

*Do not let what you cannot do interfere with what you
can do.*

— John Wooden, college basketball coach

ever attended, I promise you that if you've discovered your mission and are passionate about it—and if all the ruinous negative programming is gone from your system—and if you've given yourself *permission to win* and will apply yourself to achieving your goals by learning everything you can from every reliable source you can— your graduation certificate in life fulfillment is going to read *summa cum laude*!

When I review a seminar with audience participation, the number one thing they tell me they get from the day is the message to <u>flush it</u>! The whole negative past—<u>flush it</u>! They've learned they have to get the negativity out of their subconscious. Those old tapes don't have anything to do with who they are today and what they can achieve.

Act on that message right now! Not only are you getting rid of your negative tapes relating to learning and education, but you're doing the same thing with <u>all</u> of your negative tapes relating to each and every area of your life. The whole negative, December 31st portfolio goes into the hopper. The whole miserable package. *Flush it!*

And in the future, if negativity unexpectedly pops out at you from some hiding place in your mind, repeat the process. You'll be your own coach and you'll have the same responsibility I have. Don't let negativism linger. That's by far the most important of your self-coaching assignments.

Okay ... now let's put that behind us and get on with the positive. Let's get on with January 1st thinking!

Winners like you are always learning. Always sharpening their axes. Fine-tuning themselves. They never stop. They never reach the point where they think there's no one out there who can give them new ideas or show them better ways to do things. *They know that none of us is as smart as all of us.*

To learn what they need to learn, winners reach out to the incredibly huge world of collective knowledge—to experts, libraries, seminars, workshops, professional associations, universities, community colleges, the Internet. They read. They absorb. They listen to tapes at home and in the car. And they choose all their educators and sources carefully, getting recommendations from people who know the field. They make sure they're coached by the very best—top people with real-world experience. Then they take it all in. And they start enjoying every minute of it. It's not work. It's exciting! They're getting somewhere!

Recently, a close friend told me about a young man who writes for an advertising agency. It's a good job. He loves the work. It's exactly what he wants to do in life. But until a few years ago, he wasn't allowed to write ads for the agency's biggest and most important clients. These jobs always went to the older, more experienced pros in the company. That is, until he did something about it.

When his boss offhandedly mentioned that a huge tire manufacturer was considering their agency (the agency had to make a presentation in three months), the young man decided to act. He went to his local community college library and borrowed reference books, newsletters, and articles on the tire industry. Every spare moment for ten weeks, he learned everything he could

---

Don't look back. Someone might be gaining on you. When you look back, you know how long you've been going and that just might stop you from going any farther.

— Satchel Paige, first black pitcher in the Major Leagues

about tires and what was happening in the business. He cut out tire ads from newspapers and magazines, went to tire stores and asked questions, and even arranged to get videos from two tire companies. At the end of the ten weeks, he handed in a 15-page marketing plan to his boss to help the agency make the presentation.

His boss was flabbergasted! Nobody in the agency had anything like the knowledge evident in this report—and he used almost every bit of the report in the agency's presentation to assure the client that the agency knew what it was talking about.

The agency got the account. The young man was immediately assigned to it as the head writer. And his salary didn't double– it _tripled_! Now, that's a classic example of tapping learning sources and truly "getting somewhere."

Hey, what about you? Can you learn more about your job in your spare time? It's not your employer's responsibility to give you a better education. It's _your_ responsibility! Why not make yourself more valuable to your employer by acquiring more knowledge? Could a little study and determination make a difference? Can you do what it takes to move up the ladder? I believe you owe it to yourself and to your employer. I'll have a lot more to say about this in my chapter on the Professional spoke, but I can tell you now that getting the information you need to make _permission to win_ work in your job—and in every area of your life—is up to you, and it's all around you. It's everywhere.

And do you know what the exciting part is? It's knowing that every minute you learn, you're doing some-

---

Being ignorant is not so much a shame as being unwilling to learn to do things the right way.
— Benjamin Franklin, American inventor/statesman

thing that puts you ahead of where you were. There's no standing in place with learning. It's always pushing you forward. Learning is an investment—in yourself and in your future.

That's exciting! *That's* getting somewhere! You want to go!

One thing to keep in mind is that learning is cumulative. You never know when it will finally take hold and give you the breakthrough result you want. It takes time. Be patient.

Zig Ziglar—the master professional who shared his expertise with me and helped me so much in the early days of my career—tells a great story about the bamboo tree. The seed of the bamboo tree is planted, fertilized and watered. Nothing happens for the first year. There's no sign of growth. Not even a hint.

The same thing happens—or doesn't happen—the second year. And then the third year. The tree is carefully watered and fertilized each year, but nothing shows. No growth. No anything.

For eight years this can continue. Eight years!

Then—after the eight years of fertilizing and watering have passed, with nothing to show for it—the bamboo tree suddenly sprouts and grows thirty feet in three months!

Learning is like the bamboo tree. Studying feeds your mind with knowledge and gives it strength; there are good, healthy things steadily going on inside your head. But it may take a while before you can see it—

Every man is enthusiastic at times. One man has enthusiasm for 30 minutes, another for 30 days, but it is the man who has it for 30 years who makes a success of his life.
— Edward B. Butler, American scientist

before it all comes together into the knowledge package you need. Then, one day, it suddenly all blossoms for you. Suddenly you get it. There it is! That's it!

You may have spent hundreds of days wondering if you were getting anywhere, but all the time, one piece of information at a time, you were gradually building up to the result you were shooting for. Keep in mind what I said earlier: *overnight success takes time.*

So, be patient. No matter what your dream is, you'll probably have to reach it one step at a time. I know you believe in your dream. That means you know you'll get there! So no matter how long it takes, no matter how outrageous your dream may seem to others—no matter how remote it may seem even to you—every second of your hard work and patience is bound to pay off.

Let me give you an incredible example of patience—a man who believed in his dream and spent nearly two decades learning how to accomplish it:

I was speaking at a conference in Key West, Florida, one night and the president of the company that hired me gave me a beautiful pen as a gift. Written in gold on that pen were the words: *Today's the day!* I would come to learn that those words had been the battle cry of Mel Fisher—the famous Key West treasure hunter—during his seventeen-year search for the sunken Spanish ship, *Nuestra Señora de Atocha.*

On September 6, 1622, this heavily laden galleon of King Philip IV's fleet struck a reef in a raging storm near the Florida Keys. More than 260 people perished, and tons of gold, silver, and other precious cargo went to the

---

I learned in football that you shouldn't try to score on every play. Get the first downs and the touchdowns will hit you in the face.

— Jack Kemp, former NFL quarterback; U.S. Congressman

bottom. All attempts to locate the sunken ship had failed until the primary portion of the cargo was discovered by Mel's Treasure Salvors, Inc. on July 20, 1985.

Finding sunken treasure had been Mel's lifelong dream, and for those seventeen years it had been especially focused on the *Atocha*. Was it a crazy dream? It seemed that way to others. To secure financing for his venture Mel had to look into the eyes of wary would-be investors and persuade them to believe as he believed. It wasn't easy. In fact, it got to the point where he couldn't even pay his crew, and the only way he could motivate them to stay on the job was to encourage them by ship-to-shore telephone. Every day, from his base on shore, Mel would speak softly into the phone to his crew: *"Today's the day ... today's the day ... "*

For seventeen years he did this while his crew criss-crossed the search area, studying the charts, consulting 16th-century information and logs, trying one thing and then another, changing strategies as needed and gaining whatever knowledge they could from their countless ocean-bottom explorations of possible sites. It was an intense learning process. Frustrating. Discouraging. Almost impossible to get accurate information. But, again and again, day after day, Mel would be on the phone urging them forward: *"Today's the day ... "*

Then, one morning, after all those years of searching and learning and heartbreak, after all those years of begging for funds and pleading with people to believe in his "outrageous" dream, the words came back from the boat: *"Today's the day!! Today is the day! We found it, Mel! We found it!! It's all there!!!"*

Think of it! After all those years! As another Mel is famous for saying (Mel Allen, former broadcaster for the New York Yankees), *"How about that!"*

Mel Fisher, as you can imagine, is now a multimillionaire. His extraordinary patience—his absolute conviction in the accomplishment of his dream, his refusal to be discouraged, his willingness to learn step-by-step and tirelessly dig for the reliable information he needed—Mel Fisher's whole mental package was that of the winner.

Your dream might not be as exotic as Mel's, and you may not have to exercise seventeen years of patience to learn how to accomplish it, but you <u>do</u> need the same mental package. Buried down deep in your soul is a motherlode of hope, knowledge, and success. *Today's the day!* Go for it!

(Postscript: Mel and his wife lost their son, their daughter-in-law and one crew-member during the search for the Atocha. They perished at sea. They believed in Mel's dream; it had become their own, and they paid the ultimate price. Sometimes dreams are expensive.

When I was first touched by Mel's story, his level of commitment and persistence became my goal. Someday, I promised myself, I would have one of the coins that were recovered from the Atocha. Today I've fulfilled that promise to myself, and I wear the coin on a chain around my neck as a constant reminder to seize the day—to remember that <u>today is the day.</u> It helps me remember something else, too. It helps me to never forget that sometimes, as in Mel's case, all it takes is all you've got.

Mel would gladly put the treasure back into the sea if it would reverse the tragedy that took place, but those who were lost had been given one of life's most precious and positive gifts: Mel had taught them how to dream and how to believe. If I die chasing my dream, I could ask no more of this life, and I'd die with a smile on my face.)

Education, in itself, can be a very important mission—and, indeed, there are many who make it their mission. Learning, after all, is about growing. It's understanding yourself and the world around you. The more you know, the more you're empowered in life and the better you'll feel about yourself. Your self-esteem will be higher. You'll be more interesting. You'll feel more comfortable in every kind of company.

And you gain much, much more than that! Your job opportunities will be greater. More doors will be opened to you. You'll have a new awareness of what the world has to offer and how the system works ... new views ... more answers ... more knowledge about career options. In every way, a solid general education is a great blessing that pays big benefits in every area of your life. It's one of the most worthy of all ambitions. *You can't lose by learning!*

Recently I was talking with a waitress in one of the restaurants near my home, and she told me she had made a decision to go to school one night a week. She wanted to leave her job and acquire the skills to do something else. She wasn't sure what that "something else" would be, but she wanted to explore various courses, expand her horizons and opportunities, and free herself from waitressing. She was very, very excited.

And so was I. She's giving herself permission to look for gold. She's a winner already. You've heard it said that a journey of a thousand miles begins with

---

To find out what one is fitted to do and to secure an opportunity to do it is the key to happiness.
— John Dewey, American philosopher/educator

one step. She's taking that step—a first step toward a more fulfilling life, a life that will open up to her as she starts to gain knowledge. *Knowledge is power— personal power—the kind that enables us to see new potentials for ourselves and make them real.* For her, the entrance to that knowledge is one night a week in night school. But I believe it will be the most important door she'll ever walk through in her life.

There are two things about learning that are important to know—whether you're learning for the sake of learning or for the purpose of obtaining specific new skills or upgrading old ones. First, learning is a lifelong project. You can never learn more than you need. I believe that <u>everyone</u> has a responsibility to themselves to learn and to keep learning ... to constantly better themselves ... to realize not only their best, but their <u>very</u> best.

And second, even if you have no money, you have to find a way to make learning happen. No more excuses! You can't wait for learning to come to you. You have to get it for yourself. YOUGOTTAWANNA— the 13-letter magic word. Let me tell you about a young man who understood that perfectly:

He's the husband of a friend of mine, but at the time of this story he was a junior in high school. He lived in the South, there was no money in his family, and more than anything else he wanted to go to the University of Alabama. He wanted it so much, in fact, that he decided to go straight to the governor of the state. He telephoned the governor, arranged to visit

---

Education is a social process. Education is growth. Education is not preparation for life...education is life itself.
— John Dewey, American philosopher/educator

with him for a few minutes, and told him of his great desire to attend the finest university in existence. *"Could you help me, sir?"*

Well, the governor said he appreciated the young man's gumption and he'd see what he could do.

A short time later, the university requested a transfer of the young man's transcripts—and he ended up getting a four-year free ride at the university!

Now, admittedly, that is an exceptional story. But what is <u>not</u> exceptional are the results you can get when you're determined to get the education you want and are determined enough to be creative and make it happen. This young man <u>seized</u> the education he wanted. Since then, he's been the president of several banks. He's a community leader. He's a true winner!

Like I said—*yougottawanna!*

Learning doesn't always involve going back to classes. I've already alerted you to the countless sources of non-school information available to you in these incredibly information-filled times ... everything from libraries, cassette tapes, and the Internet to local seminars and face-to-face talks with the pros in your field.

Army General Norman Schwarzkopf, commander of the Allied Forces in the Persian Gulf War, was asked how he learned to be so victorious. He explained that often it came from carefully noting his mistakes and the mistakes of others—and not repeating them!

So, learning can come in many ways and from all directions. You just have to be alert. And the thing is, you <u>are</u> alert when you're focused on your dream and your goals. You'll be surprised how attuned you'll be to everything that might be of help to you. Your mind and senses will automatically pick up on such things—from conversations, news reports, articles, and other sources. The more focused you are, the more attuned you'll be. In other words, you'll be more interested—and that's the key to informal, day-to-day learning. It's nothing you plan. It will just happen.

Thomas Edison, perhaps the foremost American inventor of the past century (he patented the phonograph, for example, and the practical light bulb), had a grand total of <u>three months</u> of formal education! <u>Everything</u> Edison achieved was from day-to-day learning! He was focused on almost anything that had to do with electricity—he was alert to developments, tuned in to the subject, and dedicated to finding new ways of using electric energy. And his inventive talent did the rest.

The message is clear: Learning is wholly and entirely up to you. Depending on your goals, it may require classes and formal study, or it may not, but it will <u>always</u> require your dedication and commitment! And that can arise only when you have a definite objective and have given yourself the *permission* to achieve it.

Right now, you have every one of those necessary requirements. You have an objective—the best possible objective. It's the fulfilling of your dream ... the fulfilling of who you are and what you were meant to do. Objectives don't come any better than that! And because you've given yourself *permission to win,* you are automatically dedicated and committed to achieving the learning that will enable you to reach that objective.

So, it will happen for you. It can't be any other way. Not for you. Your great gift to yourself—*permission to win*—doesn't allow for any other result.

It's all yours. It's all out there for you. You will achieve your goals. You will achieve your dream. Right now, it's a promissory note. You need to take care of some learning before you can collect—but learn you will and collect you will!

Don't let anyone tell you that the only sure things in life are death and taxes. When you give yourself *permission to win*, you <u>are</u> a winner!

And that, friend, is <u>sure</u>!

When Aristotle was asked how much educated men were superior to those uneducated, he said, "As much as the living are to the dead."

— Ray J. Groves, Chairman, Ernst & Whinney

7

COMMUNICATING—THE HUB OF THE WHEEL

I understand winners. I surround myself with their company as often as possible and I've learned that no matter what their particular field of accomplishment may be, they all have certain fundamental disciplines in common. One of the most important of these shared disciplines is the ability to communicate successfully.

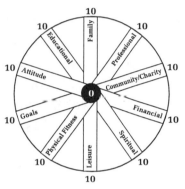

You're a winner, *so you too can expect to share that vital discipline.* In fact, your winner's attitude is automatically going to make you a better communicator. Why? Because there will be a whole new world of positive things going on inside your head. You'll be so determined to understand more, and to be understood by others, in order to accomplish your purposes, that clear, distinct two-way communication will be an instinctive priority.

Let me put it this way: *Because you are a winner, I believe you will be continually mindful of the principles of successful communication and that you will coach yourself into applying them.*

What are these principles?

Thinking before you speak. Learning how to express yourself. Learning how to listen. Understanding and paying attention to body language. Respecting other viewpoints and learning how to profit from them. Maintaining responsible control over your emotions so as not to undermine your message and success. Learning to be patient, positive, attentive, open-minded and perceptive.

Paying attention to these principles can improve your communication skills beyond anything you ever thought possible. As a winner, you <u>need</u> to do all of these things to establish effective communication and accomplish your goals. For that reason, you'll <u>want</u> to do them. Therefore, you <u>will</u> do them. It's the best thing you can do to help yourself win.

Everything you do in life involves communication. The better you communicate with family, friends, and those in your workplace, the more you'll achieve. A coach, for example, needs to communicate with his assistant coaches. He needs to communicate with his players and with the athletic director and sports information director. He needs to communicate with the press. In fact, the <u>key</u> to coaching is effective communication. The key to being a great parent is communication. The key to success in <u>any</u> business and <u>any</u> relationship is communication.

In coming chapters, I'll talk about specific methods of communication, such as within the family and in the workplace, but the overall subject of communication is so basic to achieving balance and fulfillment in your entire "Circle of Life" that the fundamental ground rules deserve this chapter of their own.

Communicating with yourself—positively!

The greatest communication skill of all is positive communication with yourself.

Mentally laying out your plans, ideas and strategies—doing it lucidly and taking time to think everything through—is the most critical communication ability you can achieve.

For a period in my life I kept a daily journal—writing down my thoughts, plans, and emotions—and it's revealing to go over that journal many years later and see how my thinking became more organized and focused as I struggled toward achievement.

In the beginning, my communication with myself had been sloppy and ill-defined, often negative, and had invariably left me floundering and confused. Not having defined my goals, I couldn't achieve them. It was like throwing darts against a blank wall. I didn't have a target to aim at. No bulls-eye to hit. I couldn't explain my goals to others. I didn't know where to get the information and help I needed. I didn't even know <u>what</u> I needed. I didn't know what direction I had to follow. I didn't know how to begin my journey toward fulfillment.

Later, however, as my positive self-communication improved and I was able to define my goals, targets, and strategies, I found that it went hand-in-hand with success and that I was consistently hitting bulls-eyes.

It's true that even in the beginning, when my self-communication was at its poorest, I was nevertheless fully aware of my mission in life—I had already figured that out—but I hadn't taken the time to seriously organize my thoughts and purposes, and I was still playing a loser's game. I was still thinking like most of the world thinks—a thought here, an idea there, a vague plan in the back of my head. It was a *wouldn't-it-be-nice-to-do-this* kind of attitude. It was <u>wishing</u>—not <u>winning</u>.

But then, a strange thing started to happen. Because I had given myself *permission to win,* the sharp distinction between wishing and winning began to dawn on me and take hold. It was nothing I planned. It just grew in my psyche. It was automatic. Increasingly, as I pondered my dreams and thought good things for myself, *my winner's attitude would not allow me to wish in vain. It insisted on results.*

Bit by bit, my whole thought process began to instinctively reorganize itself into more definite, positive, and purposeful files. I gradually found myself thinking in straighter lines. How do I <u>really</u> get from here to there? <u>Exactly</u> what will it require? What are my specific goals and strategies? It was a complete change in my method of thinking—and it was <u>action</u>-oriented. As a winner, I knew I could do what I believed I could do. Belief was no longer just an intellectual exercise. I <u>can</u> accomplish it! I <u>will</u> accomplish it! This understanding, in itself, started to discipline my thinking. I was going to <u>do</u> what I had in mind, so my plans and strategy and goals had better be well thought out!

I repeat that this new way of thinking was more instinctive than deliberate. My <u>winning self</u> was communicating with me loud and clear. It was forcing the issue. It made me <u>need</u> to think things through. It was as if I had suddenly grown up. *Permission to win* had changed everything that went on in my head.

And it will do the same in your head.

I believe that as your winner's identity begins to assert itself you are going to communicate with yourself in an organized way that leads directly to accomplishing your goals and your dreams. It may start to happen right now ... or in a few weeks ... or a few months. But because each day is January 1st and each day you renew your *permission to win,* it will indeed happen.

So be ready for it. Expect to experience a whole new era of positive self-communication. It will come. Not too long from now you'll find that you have little tolerance for wishful thinking that can't be strategized into winning results. You can wish and dream all you want—it's great; I strongly advise it!—but now you'll find your wishing focused and you'll be intent on making it happen. That's the big difference between wishing and winning. Your wishes don't stay wishes—they come true.

Effective, positive self-communication—organizing your wishing into a realistic, can-do strategy—is just the first of the many built-in benefits of giving yourself *permission to win.*

Communicating with others

Successful communication with other people involves a laundry list of ground rules. Many of them are just common sense: Be polite. Positive. Attentive. Well-groomed. Don't interrupt. And so on. You know all of these things.

But there are trickier elements to be aware of, and you'll have to continually remind yourself of them.

First of all, it's been said that 80% of <u>successful</u> communication lies in listening, observing, and determining the other person's viewpoint. Only 20% of successful communication involves <u>your</u> talking.

Before I give a keynote address or seminar, I always do a tremendous amount of research on the audience. I talk one-on-one with representative members of that audience to find out what's in their minds and where they're coming from. Sometimes I do this months in advance and then again just before the event, really digging into their attitudes, problems, and expectations. If it's a business group, I'll also review their industry and their market, and study trends and other useful data.

You see, when it comes time to give my talk, I have a very important message that I want them to understand and accept. If I am to be successful, I have to know how to approach them. I need to know how they feel and think about things. I need to know the potential obstacles I may face in getting my message across. I can't just stand up there on the stage and blurt out information at them. I'd just be talking to myself. I have to talk <u>with</u> them, not at them.

If I want to communicate effectively, I have to understand <u>their</u> viewpoint, <u>their</u> business, and <u>their</u> problems. I have to present my message in a way that will make perfect sense to <u>them</u>. *People don't care how much you know until they know how much you care.* My research shows not only how much I know but, because I've dug into their personal feelings and thoughts, it shows how much I care—and it sets the stage to give me a winning edge.

Does all this pre-seminar exploration and preparation take up a lot of my time on a project? Sure it does. About 80% of it—just as expected. The other 20% is spent in actually giving my seminar.

But it gets the results I want!

And what I want is to give them permission to win. I want them to win!

Whatever your goals and dreams are, they will involve communication with other people. Regardless of who those people are—family members, business as-

sociates, strangers who can help you—never forget that
each one of them may see things a little differently than
you do. And you will have to deal with it. Chances are,
you won't always have the advantage of predetermining
the viewpoints of the people you'll be talking with. But
that's okay. When you need cooperation from someone
you know nothing about, you still have an opportunity
to get a good feel for that person's views and learn how
you should proceed—if you do your homework.

For example, let's suppose you're in a full-time
job and one of your goals is to take an off-campus course
in psychology—something you can do by mail.

You apply to a top school and they ask you to
come for an interview before they'll sign you up. You
want the course because your mission is to be a marriage counselor. You believe in marriage. You want to
save marriages. You want to show married couples how
to reconcile their problems and live together rather than
divorce and go their separate ways. The world needs a
lot more of that kind of counseling. But what you don't
know is that the person who'll interview you hears that
same philosophy from hundreds of applicants and thinks
it's shallow ... juvenile ... not in tune with modern
times. In fact, the interviewer believes that most problem marriages <u>should</u> be dissolved.

Because you have no idea what the interviewer
thinks—you don't know anything at all about his or her
beliefs and theories—your first challenge is to find out.
Rather than blurt out your own specific theories when
you're asked, *"Why do you want to be a marriage counselor?"*, the better course would be to give a general
answer. You might say that you're aware of the chaos
in many of today's marriages—you see it among your
friends every day—and you've decided that you want

to devote your life to easing that chaos. *"I have the will to do it,"* you explain, *"but I need the training and the academic degree to pursue it. Marriage counseling is a complicated profession. I need to learn many things."*

With an approach like that, you aren't revealing the specific direction you want to follow in counseling. You aren't taking the chance of crossing swords with the one person whose approval you absolutely need at this stage. Your interviewer should agree with your answer to the question that was asked—there's nothing to <u>disagree</u> with. Most important, it gives the interviewer an irresistible temptation to express his or her feelings and theories about marriage counseling because you're obviously open to guidance—and how can the interviewer resist opening up and offering you a few opinions?

From that point forward, you know who you're dealing with. You've found out how the interviewer feels about things. You know what to say and what to avoid to guarantee successful communication. Your chances of being accepted for off-campus study have suddenly increased dramatically!

80% listening. 20% talking. That is effective communicating. Most people practice it the other way around, and that's their trouble. Suppose you had spent 80% of the interview time talking about your burning desire to save marriages—how far would that have taken you in the situation I just gave you? Instead, you felt out the interviewer's viewpoint, and potentially disastrous communication was turned into effective, result-getting communication. All it took was your awareness that you might be encountering a different point of view and your willingness to proceed cautiously until you discovered what it was.

You can use the same strategy in any situation where you're communicating with someone you know nothing about. Start slowly and feel out the other person's viewpoint before going ahead blindly. It pays off. (By the way, that example I used is the real-life account of a young sales rep in Maine. He'll be getting his B.A. in psychology next year.)

Even when you and someone else are basically on the same wavelength—with mutual interests—there can still be different ways of seeing the same thing.

In my seminars, I'll often put a chair in the middle of the stage. I'll put several objects on the chair, such as a pen, car keys, rings, etc., and then I'll ask a few participants to come up and stand at different positions around the chair. I ask them to cover one eye with their hand and pretend they're looking at the chair through a knothole in a fence. Then I ask them to tell me what they see.

Remember, they're all looking at the same thing— but each is looking at it from a different position. To one participant, the keys are closer than the rings. To another, the rings are closer. To still another, from his or her particular position, the pen might be hidden behind the keys—it isn't in sight at all. And so on. Each participant is focused on the same chair with the same items on it, but each sees something different. In fact, one person can see only the back of the chair—unable to see any of the items!

That's the way it is in real life—everyone looks at the same things through different knotholes and gets a different perspective on what they see. And sometimes they don't see anything at all, even if it's perfectly noticeable to everyone else.

That's why it's vitally important to slow down when we try to communicate—to take the time to listen and view things through the other person's knothole. It's not a question of someone being right or wrong. From your perspective, you're right. From the other person's perspective, he or she is right. Everyone is sincere and truthful. But you can see how productive communication could quickly break down if you didn't understand the other person's viewpoint and insisted on presenting everything from your viewpoint.

How much better it is to go slowly, to listen and determine where the other person's views are coming from. By respectfully taking those views into account, you can accomplish miracles in communication.

The bottom line is that you must be a good communicator to get the help and support you need to achieve your goals and dreams. That's an unavoidable fact. And the more you can learn about the other person's feelings and views before you start talking, the better prepared you'll be to communicate effectively.

So, make it a rule: *when you've got something to say, begin by listening.*

How do you express yourself? When it's your turn to talk, are your thoughts organized and clear? Have you done what we discussed earlier? Have you communicated with yourself beforehand so that you're focused—or are you going to stumble around with half-formed thoughts and confuse the person you're talking to? Hey, we've all been guilty of that. But remember: as your winning attitude takes over it will instinctively coach you into better communicating habits.

You can't win by presenting confused messages, and after you've experienced a couple of needless setbacks the winner in you will start to clarify your communication in a hurry! You can count on it! It gives you the winner's edge.

Expressing yourself clearly also means that you'll clarify anything that might be interpreted in a way you don't mean. Remember the knotholes. What's plainly self-evident to you may be ambiguous to someone else—they may see it slightly differently. The rule here is not to trust to luck. Explain what you mean. If you still doubt that your meaning is understood, you might try to bring your point into the conversation more than once, perhaps from a different angle. You also can ask the other person if they have any questions about the things you've said. A little care in this situation can save a lot of subsequent confusion.

I frequently repeat this sentence to myself as a reminder of what I always need to do when I talk to others: *KISS—Keep It Simple, Simon!*

I say "Simon" because in this game, as in the "Simple Simon" game, I have to take orders—only this time from myself. I'm ordering myself to speak in simple terms that everyone can understand.

You see, most great communication is absolutely simple. It can be understood by anyone. One of the best examples of this is Abraham Lincoln's "Gettysburg Address." It was brief, to the point, absolutely clear—and disdained by his critics as being in common language and unworthy of an American president. Yet, it lives in history because it was expressed in simple terms and with deep feelings that everyone understood.

There was another speaker at Gettysburg that day—the noted orator, Edward Everett. In fact, he was the featured speaker (Lincoln's attendance being an afterthought). Everett spoke extravagantly for two hours. Lincoln spoke for less than three minutes. Yet few people have ever expressed themselves more nobly than President Lincoln did on that occasion. Everett later wrote to him: *"I should be glad if I could flatter myself that I came as near to the central idea of the occasion in two hours as you did in two minutes."*

Winston Churchill spoke in the simplest of terms, in the language of the people, and moved the free world to Britain's cause. Jesus frequently used parables for clarity and spoke in Koine, a dialect of Greek. The word *"Koine"* itself means "common"—*"koine dialectos"* means "common language."

And who was more a master of plain speaking than Harry Truman? No one ever misunderstood where he was coming from, and to this day there is nostalgia for such simplicity and unconfused directness in communication by our leaders. You don't have to like what you hear, but you can't help but like simplicity, plainness, and clarity. These are the keys to expressing yourself effectively.

When I present information about communication in my programs, I have people pair up and then ask them a series of questions and give them assignments. One of the assignments is that they must speak to their partner as if they were eight years old. They must speak in eight-year-old language and with no business talk or big words.

They love it! The energy is really high in the room. But, most important, they learn that when they speak as simply as possible there is never any confusion in anyone's mind about what is being said. Everyone understands everyone else.

Here they are, all grown up, educated and sophisticated in the ways of the world—and yet the best way to be sure they're understood by everyone at all times is to return to the simple, nonambiguous language of childhood!

Boy, how we have lost those skills! I see it every day wherever I go—from the corner store to corporate board rooms. Countless millions of words are spoken, but only a fraction are understood. The people who are trying to communicate don't understand what I tell myself every day: *"KISS—Keep It Simple, Simon!"*

People can be impressed by what you know only if you express your thoughts in a way they can understand. When you realize that—and practice it—you are giving yourself one of the greatest tools of winning.

When you communicate, hoping for cooperation and understanding, do you make the common mistake of asking people to read your mind? Never assume that people will automatically help you to achieve your goals when they don't know anything about your long-range plans and your spirit and dedication to your dream. That's a part of you they need to know about.

By and large, most people want to be helpful, and especially so when they meet up with a person of commitment and purpose. *Help them help you* by opening up your mind to them and telling them about your total game plan.

When you ask someone to help you achieve a goal (for example, you might ask a community college counselor to recommend a good phys-ed program that leads to a degree), the counselor might think little of it. But when you reveal the big picture, that your end mission is to coach the handicapped, the counselor may suggest all kinds of helpful ideas and suggestions. He or she may alert you to specialized courses, seminars, associations, and other sources of information, help, and guidance that it might otherwise have taken you months or years to learn about. It's amazing what people might do for you once they know what's on your mind.

But they won't know unless you tell them. And you have to tell them in a way they'll understand.

Sincerity

Another absolute essential in effective communicating is <u>sincerity</u>. Even if the other person disagrees with your viewpoint, your sincerity is likely to be highly respected and can often be instrumental in eventually changing the opinions of those who initially oppose you. Without sincerity—real, from-the-heart, take-your-mask-off sincerity—very little is accomplished in communication and your words will not be taken seriously.

I once heard my pastor tell this story:

Many years ago, a man was famous for walking across Niagara Falls on a tightrope, guiding a wheelbarrow in front of him. He had performed this feat many, many times, but on one particular day he thought the wind was blowing too hard, so he canceled his act.

Well, a large crowd had gathered and they were disappointed. They egged him on, telling him he could make it.

"Do you really believe I can make it?" he asked. *"Do you <u>really</u> believe I can make it?"*

"Yeah!" they all shouted. *"Go for it! You can make it!"*

The man smiled and turned to the nearest person in the crowd. *"Do <u>you</u> believe I can make it?"*

"You bet!" said the man. *"I believe you can make it."*

"Okay," said the daredevil, *"then you get in the wheelbarrow."*

When you want people to believe in you and take you seriously, you have to get in the wheelbarrow. No matter what your message is, lack of sincerity and conviction is probably the easiest thing to spot in a person, and countless people have been denied help because of it.

That's not going to happen to you—I believe you'll think out your goals and dreams carefully and will be sincerely committed to them. Your winner's attitude will not allow you to wimp out. You're better than that. And it will show.

I believe you'll also appreciate the next thing my pastor said to me to wrap up his wheelbarrow story: *"Your life speaks so loudly I can't hear what you're saying."*

Body Language

You've heard about body language. When you're talking with someone, you hear that person's words, but you can often tell more about how they're <u>really</u> reacting to your message by their facial expressions and how they look at you, or even by their posture and how they sit or stand. That's called "body language"—the nonverbal signals a person sends that give you clues as to how successfully you're communicating.

Excellent books have been written about body language—and it's well worth your time to read up on the subject—but I believe you can usually interpret another person's real feelings instinctively. At some point in a conversation, you can usually tell whether the other person is open to your message. It's a sense most of us have. You may not know the fine points of interpreting body language, but if the other person is disinterested, you'll sense it. If the other person is untruthful, you'll sense it. If you're wasting your time, you'll sense it.

Whatever leads you to such conclusions, I believe they're mostly arrived at through your senses, and I've long been persuaded that it's best to trust your senses.

Be alert to body language, but don't get too up-tight about it. For example, if the body language of the other person doesn't fit the words you're hearing—if you sense a contradiction between that person's words and their expression or posture—you'll be aware of it and you'll suspect that there's probably a communications problem. But maybe there isn't. Body language isn't a perfect science. Let your instincts take over. Some people's body language, for instance, can display all of the so-called "good signs" that are supposed to encourage you. They'll give you a firm handshake, look you straight in the eye, be totally attentive—and be the most two-faced humans alive. On the other hand, some people who are sincerely interested in you and really listening to you the most closely might be walking around the room and staring out the windows—it's just the way they do their best listening and thinking.

A few months ago, I needed to accomplish a very complex and long-standing goal. It was crucial to me. I'd been told about a man who could help me, but I'd never met him, so I set up a meeting.

During our meeting, he <u>always</u> looked around at everything but me. He'd fidget and tie his shoelaces, or he'd get up and pour a cup of coffee, or he'd stare up at the trees (we were sitting outside). If there was a lull in the conversation, he'd talk about my car or his girl-friend or something else that was way off of the subject at hand. Sometimes, when he was sitting, I got the notion he was half asleep.

In short, nothing in this man's body language made me believe for a minute that he was interested in a word I was saying. Yet I somehow sensed I could count on him to give me the help and expertise I was after. I just <u>felt</u> it.

It was amazing. Months later, this man's recall of our conversation was total. He'd taken it all in—even things I'd forgotten. His perception of what I needed was <u>outstanding</u>. He'd gotten it exactly right. And the job he did for me enabled me to accomplish my goal far better than I had ever thought possible.

So what did this tell me? It told me not to be too exact about trying to interpret body language—and I pass that lesson along to you now as your coach. Let your senses be your guide. Trust them. Usually, deep down, you'll just <u>know</u> whether you're communicating successfully. It's instinctive. That's the most useful real-life rule I can give you.

As for your own body language, common sense applies. Obviously, you should present yourself as competently as you can manage. And by that I mean you should be positive, well-groomed, pleasant, attentive, respectful, mindful of the things we've talked about in this chapter—and above all, of course, you should be well prepared and absolutely sincere. If you have those things going for you, I believe your body language will reflect it.

In light of this, I don't think my pastor would mind if I went back and made a slight change in his great little homily: *"Your <u>body language</u> speaks so loudly I can't hear what you're saying."*

Emotions and Tone

Your emotions and your tone of voice play a part in successful communicating.

Your enthusiasm for a project may often seem overblown to others who don't share your particular dream—and that's understandable. <u>Some</u> enthusiasm is obviously demanded, but it has to be tempered with quiet sincerity and clear evidence that you've thought your project out carefully and realistically. If you have lots of enthusiasm and little substance, your enthusiasm won't mean much to the other person. But if your enthusiasm is matched by substance, it will make sense and can often be impressive.

"Tone of voice" involves not only decibel range, but also your style—that is, whether your tone is friendly, businesslike, humorous, down-to-earth, worldly, and so on. In this chapter—where we're talking about the general rules of communicating in respect to achieving your mission (which means mostly you'll be looking for help from strangers and others you don't know very well)—a combination of friendly and businesslike is the preferable way to start out.

If the person you're talking with gets right to the point, do the same. If you see signs of humor, join in guardedly. Take your cue from the other person. He or she will set the atmosphere, and you'll both be more comfortable on a common wavelength. Be cautious. Use your good sense. Remember—you don't know each other all that well, and it's best to be familiar just to the extent offered by the other person.

Raising your voice unnecessarily can be interpreted as a sign of anger or frustration and is to be avoided in every instance. Keep focused on your goal and the reason you're having the meeting; don't sabotage it by losing control. A decision about helping you—or not helping you—may often be made after a meeting is over, and it can sometimes be favorable simply because the other person was aware that you had kept a rein on your feelings.

Once again—a little caution, some common sense, and staying focused on your mission will keep your emotions and tone in check.

What we've had here so far is a good selection of the basic ground rules for positive, effective communicating— the rules everyone is expected to follow if they want to succeed. You can liken it to the official game rules that football referees carry around in their heads. If you don't follow the fundamental rules, you're penalized. You can get away with a few infractions now and then, but not all the time. And if you're penalized often enough, it kills your chances of winning.

You want to win, so as your own communications coach you'll be upset if you kill your progress with stupid infractions. Have a firm talk with yourself—forgive yourself and learn from it—but then get on with the game.

Like any sports team, however, how you actually play the communication game—within the basic rules—is up to you. It's a matter of strategy and tactics (charge the line or go around the end, for example; punt or go for it; call "time" or hurry up). What you decide to do depends on the exact situation you're facing and how you think you can turn it into a winning play. In the next few chapters we'll do a lot of fine-tuning regarding communications options and developing strategies you can use in specific situations.

Effective communicating really is the common denominator of winners, and although it may be challenging to communicate effectively with everybody, you can make it work when and where it counts. You're a winner. You'll coach yourself into getting it right.

Remember, the responsibility for great communication lies with you. Go for it! Start right now to communicate positively with yourself and with others. Keep it simple.

And have fun!

8

FAMILY AND PERSONAL RELATIONSHIPS

In my office, we assign an "A," "B," or "C" priority to nearly everything we do. When I'm out of town and call in for my messages, I only want to know about the most urgent ones, the "A" priorities. I want to know what's most important that day and who I have to respond to first.

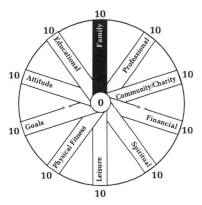

Nature has seen to it that we have a similar priority system in our minds and hearts. Under Nature's system, the "A" priority is *family and personal relationships*.

When we have a problem with someone we love, it is continually on our mind to one degree or another. There's no getting away from it—not at work, not at leisure, not at any time. Depending on the severity of the problem, our emotional reactions can range from simply a mild distraction in the back of our minds to thought-numbing grief and dysfunction. The bottom line is that when we have trouble at home and in our close relationships, it cannot be dismissed from our thoughts and emotions—it commands our attention. It's our natural and instinctive "A" priority.

Yesterday, December 31st, you may have approached your relationship problems with negative thinking. You may have attempted to put them aside. You may have fooled yourself into thinking you didn't have time to deal with personal stress. Or you may have convinced yourself you couldn't do anything about the situation. Maybe you just blamed your problems on somebody else.

But that was December 31st. Ancient history. Today is January 1st. It's time to trash your negative thinking!

Remember, only you can give yourself *permission to win*—and that means <u>unqualified</u> permission to win in <u>every</u> area of your "Circle of Life." For you, there's no such thing as choosing to be positive in one area and negative in another. You can't say to yourself, *"Well, I can win in business. But I can't win in my love life."* If you've truly given yourself *permission to win,* your winning attitude is <u>built in</u>! <u>Every</u> challenge is automatically and instinctively approached with a positive, January 1st attitude! That's the priceless gift you've given to yourself. And it means that you will <u>always</u> win in the long run.

I'm a real-world coach and I'm not talking about magic here. I'm talking about what you <u>will</u> accomplish in the infinitely complex world of relationships. I'm talking about winning when you're rejected by a loved one. Winning when your marriage has failed. Winning when your kids revolt. Winning over loneliness. Winning in the countless situations brought on by emotional stress, strife, and disappointment with those you love the most.

Winning—<u>real</u> winning—often comes in a form you don't expect. For example, someone you love walks out on you. Your solution is to win that person back. That is the victory you have in mind. You're convinced you can do it. But, try as you might, you can't make it happen. You have failed that challenge. You couldn't get that person back. Does that make you a loser?

Of course not! Were the cancer kids losers because they couldn't get their physical health back?

Winning solutions are what make you a winner <u>*despite*</u> *the outcome of a specific challenge.* The challenges are battles. You may lose some. But when you give yourself *permission to win,* you never lose the war. You survive. You go forward. And inevitably your winner's attitude provides you with victory in ways that may have never occurred to you at the start—ways that lead to real, lasting fulfillment.

I know many winners who were nearly crushed at some point in their lives by unsolvable relationship problems. They were grief-stricken, hopeless, depressed beyond the telling of it. Yet, their attitude and winning convictions would not allow them to be totally undone. These men and women had failed to win the battles in their relationships and they had to crawl up from emotional cellars. They had to turn their situation around and realize good from it. They had to find go-ahead advantages in situations that were giving them nothing but heartbreak and grief. They had lost the battle—yet their winning spirit had destined them to win the war. If they can do it, so can you!

Several years ago, the wife of a very good friend of mine announced that she was leaving him. He adored her, he had no inkling there was trouble between them (not a word), and he was devastated. It was his second marriage, and more than all else in this world he had wanted it to succeed. There were young children involved, complicating the matter, and he was immediately obsessed with preserving the marriage. He couldn't

concentrate on his work, gave up his mail-order business, agreed to marriage counseling and did everything
humanly possible to encourage his wife to stay. He was
convinced he could do it, but nothing he did was to any
avail, and within a few months his downfall was complete. His wife, family, home, and business reputation
were gone, and so were most of their mutual friends.
The wife was granted a divorce within five months and
then married a man whom she'd been seeing for the
past year.

My friend was in a severe emotional state and
immediately made the rounds of local self-help groups
to learn how to deal with his grief. He stuck with these
groups for a few weeks, but didn't find their methods
and philosophies personally appealing, so he decided
to start a group of his own.

He secured a meeting room in the basement of a
local hospital and ran an ad in the "Personals" column
inviting fellow grievers to come in on Tuesday nights
and talk about their troubles. Word got out quickly. The
meetings were friendly and informal, and within a few
weeks he'd made dozens of new friends and heard so
many accounts of emotional devastation (some much
worse than his own) that he was able to put his own
grief into perspective—the first step toward controlling it.

Equally important, he could see that his unstruc-
tured get-togethers were genuinely helping people—he
could read it in their changing attitudes and manner-
isms as they came back week after week. Depression
was being replaced by humor, empty faces took on life,
smiles replaced tears, silence was replaced by eagerness
to talk. He was involved with these people. He cared
for them. They were coping, changing, coming back to
life right before his eyes.

He didn't know it, but week by week he was beginning to win in his own situation. He was helping himself by helping others—one of the most powerful of all therapies. He was gradually coming out of the terrible place he was in. So genuinely did he progress, in fact, that after only four months he found himself less and less focused on grief and more and more focused on positive things, such as putting his mail-order business back together. He was still hurting—big time—but he was gradually regaining his ability to function.

In fact, after five months, he realized he didn't belong at the meetings, turned them over to another person, and stopped attending. He had edged back into life. He was on his way. He had given himself *permission to win* over his situation.

Today, my friend enjoys a new life and a new relationship that is infinitely more happy, productive, and fulfilling than anything he had known in the past. When he describes his devastated frame of mind in the days when he was obsessed with keeping the love of the woman who had left him, he uses an interesting word: "laughable."

He doesn't use it in a humorous way. It's just that he finds that whole December 31st scenario so unthinkable and so unimportant today that "laughable"—in the sense of astounding or amazing—is the best word for it.

It may sound strange, but many champions are made champions by setbacks. They are champions because they've been hurt. Their experience moved them and pulled out this fighting spirit, making them what they are. Sometimes in life, God gives us a difficulty in order to bring out the fighting spirit. Everything that happens to you can happen for good if you have this spirit.

— Bob Richards,
pole vaulter; two-time Olympic Gold Medalist

He looks back on his grief almost with disbelief. At the time, when no solutions worked and he was losing every battle, he couldn't have dreamed of the final victory in store for him. He couldn't have imagined how generously his will to win would provide that victory, and that it would provide it in ways he hadn't expected or calculated.

To all of you out there who have genuinely given yourself *permission to win* and are counting on it to make you a winner in the face of grief over your relationships, I promise you it will do just that. You may lose every intervening challenge, but your built-in winning attitude will bring you to final victory. It will not let you down. Under even the most emotionally devastating circumstances, it will find ways to overcome every setback.

There's an old saying that reflects that fact perfectly: *We can't adjust the wind, but we can adjust the sails.* That's exactly what a winning attitude does for you. It automatically adjusts to unavoidable circumstances and moves you forward—sometimes unexpectedly. **It maneuvers you beyond temporary defeats and, in the long run, makes you unconquerable.**

That is the heart and soul of *permission to win.* And nowhere is that permission more priceless to you than when you are grieving over great losses in family and personal relationships.

In this chapter, we'll take a look at today's complicated society and discuss ways to approach some common relationship problems with a winner's attitude.

When one door closes, another opens. But we often look so long and so regretfully upon the closed door that we do not see the one which has opened for us.
— Alexander Graham Bell, inventor/scientist

Heading off relationship problems is easier than solving them after they've become serious.

Unconditional love

This is the real heart of successful relationships with spouses, kids, and loved ones. This is where winning starts.

The greatest need an individual has is to be totally loved, regardless of whatever happens. That's unconditional love. Unconditional love cannot be qualified. Either you give it or you don't—and nothing will hurt and disillusion someone you love more than his or her awareness that you're not providing it. I believe this is the root cause of most broken marriages and relationships, and of the alienation of children from their parents. (Or parents from their children—it works both ways.)

Unconditional love is the glue that holds people together in even the toughest circumstances. It's a rare and precious commodity that can't be lightly dismissed by the person to whom it is offered. When you give it, you can be forgiven for almost everything. When you don't, it's likely you won't be forgiven for anything.

You may be convinced you're truly offering unconditional love. It may be in your heart and mind, but you may not be expressing it consistently and plainly in a way that's recognized by the other person. If you even suspect that those you love don't know how you really feel, then this is where your will to win and your champion's attitude can make the most important difference in your life.

Here are a few insights and coaching tips:

The only time I ever experienced unconditional love was from my mother. My father was wonderful and he loved me, but I didn't feel his love was the same as my mother's. I knew that no matter what, I couldn't <u>drive</u> my mother's love from me. Even if I held up a bank or killed somebody, I knew she'd still love me. I've never again encountered unconditional love like that, except from my dog, Socrates. Other people's love was always conditional. I'd be loved if I did this, or if I did that. As a consequence, I had an unhealthy attitude about love. I couldn't expect it unconditionally. I had to <u>earn</u> love. I had to <u>seek</u> it. I had to do the <u>right thing</u> to get it.

If someone you love feels that way—if they feel they have to earn your love—then your relationship is in danger. Why? Because he or she—all of us—resent having to earn love. It's hard. It's not rewarding. There's something intrinsically wrong and unfulfilling about it. What kind of love is it if we have to earn it and vie for it and if it's based on what we do rather than who we are? How deep is it? How long will it last? If we screw up, will we lose it? These are real fears.

When arguments and contentions with loved ones get out of hand and focus down on what the other person has or hasn't done, hasty words can be spoken that can make the other person doubt our unconditional love. Defensiveness sets in, then resentment, then deep hurt and doubt ... and the relationship can start to unravel. A person's need for unconditional love—one's need for the <u>sureness</u> of being loved no matter what—is so strong that the doubting party may begin to seek it elsewhere, knowingly or unknowingly. *Effectively communicating unconditional love is ESSENTIAL for solid, stable relationships.*

This doesn't mean that you blind yourself to the other person's faults. Differences of opinion, arguments, efforts to guide and correct, even criticism can be expected in every relationship. But it's necessary to take great care that they don't threaten the other person's security about your love. There are countless rules about this subject covering every conceivable situation in family and personal relationships—between adults, between adults and children, and so on—but the essential, <u>foundational rule</u> in <u>every</u> situation involving those you love is to simply understand and acknowledge their NEED for unconditional love.

Just your <u>awareness</u> of that will work wonders. It will make you cut an argument short when you sense you're going too far. It will encourage you to take a softer, more positive approach. It will lessen the anger in your voice. It will put you in the other person's shoes so you'll know when you're threatening his or her belief in your love. It'll help you do a couple of other things, too. It will help you to hug that person when the confrontation is over. It will help you to say, *"I love you."*

If you truly feel unconditional love for someone and remain continually aware of the other person's need for it, you don't need rules. Your love will dictate your words and actions. That's the surest formula for keeping relationships intact and making them invulnerable to the forces that seek to tear them apart.

Let's put it this way: it's not love that conquers all. It's <u>unconditional</u> love that conquers all. Communicating it plainly—particularly in stressful situations—is championship play at its best. Everybody wins.

Unconditional respect

This goes hand-in-hand with unconditional love, and for the moment I'll confine it only to <u>adult</u> relationships. (Lack of respect toward a child is so enormously destructive that it will have a section of its own.)

Putting down your spouse or significant other in front of <u>anybody</u>—whether within the family or outside of it—is the fast lane to a broken relationship. Believe me, the embarrassed party will remember it. Nothing is more damaging to one's sense of security, family, and togetherness than to be dishonored in front of others.

Sure, we all have our disagreements with those we love, but with patience and concern for the other's viewpoint the differences can usually be straightened out or at least accommodated. But the moment we go beyond the substance of the disagreement and start accusing the other person of being stupid or hopeless— particularly where others can hear it—we've crossed an important line: we've now shown disrespect for who that person <u>is</u>, and this gives them reason to doubt how we feel about them.

You see, when we attack the character of the other person, the issue is no longer about the disagreement we're having with them. Suddenly, it's about them as a person—the deep traits we see in them. They have every right to wonder how we can love them if we think they're stupid, hopeless, etc. Insecurity sets in. Where's that unconditional love they'd been counting on?

When we make disrespectful accusations—in public or private, perhaps sarcastically—they can be enormously destructive. It's not so much that a put-down affects the other person's self-esteem (again, leaving children out of it for the moment), but it's the raising of doubts about your unconditional love that matters the most. That's where the real harm is done to your relationship.

It goes without saying that unconditional <u>love</u> prompts unconditional <u>respect</u>. They go together. I don't know how the two can be separated, and I don't know how a relationship can survive without your effectively demonstrating these feelings in words and actions whenever you have the chance.

Kids

In our society of 50% divorce rates, latch-key kids, one-parent families, working mothers, and incredible family pressures, a home atmosphere of unconditional love and respect is vital.

Kids need a "safety zone" in a confused and complicated world. They need a place of mental comfort and security. A haven where they know they're accepted and approved. They need a place where they can stop to get their bearings and sort out the influences that are continually seeking to control them—peer pressure, movies, TV—the whole world of twisted values in which money, sexual gratification, violence, craftiness, and self-serving often assume the proportions of saintliness.

It's hard enough today for adults to maintain their own balance and self-esteem, fulfilling themselves meaningfully, when the traditional values of monogamy, decency, compassion, honest work, spiritual beliefs, and respect for others are everywhere seen as passé. If it's challenging and confusing for them, imagine what it's like for kids.

If you have school-age children, one in two of their classmates is statistically from a broken home. These kids spend half their time with two different families. They're being programmed by two different sets of family values—sometimes totally opposed values regarding such basic foundations as religion and career orientation.

If you were a kid, how would you cope with this? Who would you trust? What would you believe? How would you feel under such circumstances? Here are some words: *Confused ... resentful ... misunderstood ... alone.*

Hey, you'd find it easier to get in with a bunch of other kids, do what they do, assume their values, and wing it from there. Perhaps you really <u>were</u> one of those kids. And perhaps that's what you really did. (It's a safe assumption on my part; the odds in today's society are 50-50.)

But those odds drop dramatically *if you had a home (single-parent or otherwise) where you knew for <u>sure</u> you were unconditionally loved and accepted despite your faults and mistakes.* The odds are probably 10-1 that you wouldn't revolt if you had a home where you <u>knew</u> you were a priority ... where your parents (or parent) had real time for you ... where grown-ups actually <u>listened</u> to you and worked with you to solve your problems and answer questions ... where you had a rock-solid sense of getting proper compass directions for your life.

It's true that kids can find <u>acceptance</u> within a peer group—but they can't find all the rest of the things they instinctively yearn for. A peer group is not competitive with a Mom and/or Dad who are wise and loving enough to supply the whole package of benefits at home.

In the beginning, a child's literal and instinctive roots are at home. Mom and Dad are the leaders. The protectors. The wise ones. The comforting ones. The ones who know what's best. The ones who can really be counted on for love and understanding. It's not until that trust is broken—not until disillusionment and confusion and insecurity set in—that the child begins to look to himself, his peers, and the current mores of society for the orientation he or she lacks at home.

You say you do your best. You say you offer your child unconditional love. You don't understand why

Johnny or Susie is rebellious. You don't understand why you seem to be losing your child.

Look at it from the child's viewpoint.

To a kid, a good part of love is spelled T-I-M-E. It's often said that it's the quality of the time you spend with a kid that counts, not the quantity. That's nonsense. It's a lie perpetrated by a society that seeks to rationalize a system that forces parents to be away from their kids 90% of the time. There isn't a worthwhile mother or father on this planet who doesn't feel guilty about being absent most of the day from his or her kids. It's natural and instinctive. It's built into mothers and fathers. You know it and I know it. And all the reasons and rationale and social propaganda in the world can't change it.

The quantity of time you spend with a child is every bit as important as the quality. You have to be there for your child—whether or not you're conversing or doing something together. Just the assurance that you're around is comforting.

As a child, I was fortunate on most nights to go to bed warmed and comforted just by the fact that Mom and Dad were in the house. There was security in it. And sweet sleep. If I had a rough day in school, my troubles started disappearing the moment I came home and spotted my Mom bustling around the kitchen as she always did. It was familiar. Comforting. It was the stuff of a secure childhood. I can't tell you how many times I just sort of hung around with my Dad, not saying anything in particular, just watching and doing my own thing, maybe lending a hand with cleaning the yard, stuffing trash into a bag or just going along with him on a drive to the store. Hey, what's better than that? Not everyone's been as lucky.

All of the things I've just mentioned could be categorized as quantity time between parents and their

kids. But, to me, every moment of it is also Grade-A
quality time. Is quality time an hour of serious discussion with a kid about family togetherness? Sure. But so
is demonstrating togetherness by simply being around
the house and engaging in small-talk about birds' nests
or snowplows. Just the security of parental availability
and interest is priceless. Don't let the social apologists
kid you. Quantity time is quality time.

Unfortunately, I didn't give my own children as
much security in this area as my folks gave me. Zoraida,
the mother of my children, and from whom I'm divorced,
did a great job of making up for my lapse. At the time,
I had given in to many of the same negative pressures
influencing most of today's working parents. They're
stretched and pulled in so many different directions—the
time demands are so brutal—that the only thing they want
to do when they get home is to be left alone, chill out,
and wind down. The trouble is that the kids have also had
a challenging day and come home with a lot on their
minds—they need to process things—but the parents are
too weary to focus on it. Dinner is likely to be zapped in
the microwave, the TV turned on for news or escape, and
before you know it it's time for bed and that's it for the
day. This common scenario is compounded in a single-
parent family where the breadwinner, cook, chauffeur, and
housekeeper are usually all rolled into one, and the kids'
needs for nightly talk and guidance have to compete with
their mother's or father's sheer exhaustion.

Everything about that scene is typical. It's repeated
in countless households every day and night of the year.
And it's the kids who are being shortchanged.

It doesn't have to be that way. Let me tell you
about a single-parent situation where the kids win—and
win big! And so does the parent!

I personally know a woman in her forties (I'll call her M.B.) who was divorced three years ago and moved to rural New England with two kids aged 13 and 9. She received no alimony and had little money but, luckily, she was able to manage a successful business from her new home and generated a decent income.

The workload of her business demanded 12 hours a day of her attention, but because it was home-based she could switch many working hours to nights and weekends and make time for her kids according to their schedules. She could make the kids her number-one priority and raise them as she thought best—and her schedule was mind-boggling

Because the local school offered almost nothing in the way of decent college-prep curricula, M.B. registered them in a city school forty minutes away. She had to get up at 5:30 every morning and drive them there. She could occasionally arrange for a fill-in driver, but generally she drove both ways twice a day, a daily total of 120 miles.

Both kids were exceptionally good in sports and interested in school-connected clubs and special projects. M.B. made time for all of these needs, seeing to it that her children took part in whatever was of interest to them, and because they were of different ages and in different activities and groups, the scheduling was brutal, often requiring her to make a third daily round-trip into the city. On Sundays, she saw to it that they went to church, requiring still another trip into the city.

M.B. was also a first-class nutritionist and went to exceptional lengths to buy organically-grown food from specialty stores and co-ops. This she usually attended to after she dropped the kids off at school or when she was in the city to pick up her kids from the dentist or orthodontist, or from their various after-school activities.

On an average day, then, M.B. would spend up to six hours chauffeuring, shopping, cooking, house-cleaning, helping with homework and other projects related solely to her children. Many, many of her friends wondered how she could keep going at such a pace and still run a successful business. But she did, averaging six to seven hours of sleep each night, and the payoff was—and is—priceless.

Both of her children are honors students. Both have made the varsity squads in their chosen sports at school. Both are extremely well-liked by fellow students and have many friends. Both adore their mother and are emotionally secure, well-adjusted, and unaffected by the divorce to an extent few of us would consider possible. They are exceedingly happy, healthy, productive kids; it's a sheer pleasure to be around them. Their value systems have been nurtured with extraordinary care and they have no doubt whatever that their welfare—in every way—is the central priority in their household.

Admittedly, M.B.'s in-home business and the income it provides play a major role in this particular single-parent success story. But it's M.B.'s spirit and prioritizing that stand out the most markedly. It's the love and interest so obviously shown toward the children—and the return of that love by the children—that stands as an object lesson for every parent reading this book, regardless of their financial situation. The key isn't money—it's hard work, unselfishness, patience, and commitment.

In fact, if you're a single parent working outside the home and can't begin to give the same amount of time to your children as M.B. does, the fact that your kids <u>know</u> you are giving it to the best of your ability is enough. They need to understand that you're doing the best you can with the tools in your toolbox. But that has to be clearly communicated to them in your words and actions. They have to really believe it. If they do, it can work to unite even the poorest family in common purpose and understanding, and in mutual efforts to ease the burden.

In a town in Maine, near where my mother was born and where I love to visit, a local bank president is one of seven kids who were successfully raised on a nearby dirt farm by exceedingly hard-working, low-income parents. The most striking things about that bank president—to people who know him personally—are his reflections on his childhood and the time his parents always managed to make to guide him and his brothers and sisters.

It was dawn-to-late-night work on that small piece of rock-strewn farmland—every child from walking age up had specific chores to do; even the kids' school clothes were home-made by his or her mother and sisters—but no question or concern voiced by the children ever went unanswered. There was always time to listen to them and discuss things. The word he once used to describe the love in his household was *"magical."*

Kids can take almost anything—*if they are obviously loved and respected.* If they aren't, then every shortage and hardship can be resented. The common factor among most rebellious kids is their feeling of not being loved. It's not lack of money in the family. On the contrary, a kid often sees the parents' fixation on money as the thing he or she is <u>competing</u> with. Just look around for yourself. Likely as not, you'll see that rebellious kids usually associate with peers who don't have <u>any</u> money!

So, what it takes is love ... and, like I said, a large part of love is spelled T-I-M-E. Your children need as much of it as you can give. For example, they need a period of uninterrupted time with you when you come home from work. They know you're busy and exhausted. They can see it. But now you're home and they need to know that they're a priority.

They need that daily dose of security. They need you to <u>listen</u> to them. They need to know you're <u>interested</u> in what's going on in their lives. They know you've got your mind on a lot of other things. And that you're worried about a lot of other things. But now it's their turn. They want to feel they're as important to you as all those "other things." It's not too much to ask. Their feelings and needs aren't a burden to you. They're your <u>children</u>. They want to know that they're more important to you than the transmission that fell out of your car that morning. Or the raise you didn't get. Show them that they <u>are</u> and they'll probably charm you by offering to help you fix the transmission. Or they might offer to give up their allowance.

They love you. They <u>want</u> to help. They <u>want</u> to make things easier. They're all yours <u>if</u> they know you love and respect them, <u>if</u> you offer yourself and your time to them. They <u>have</u> to know they're a priority!

Families need fellowship—positive time together that is nurturing, constructive, fulfilling, and fun. Just hanging out together builds mutual respect and honor. It gives kids a sense of direction and identity.

My fondest memories of childhood are of family get-togethers—from going camping on vacations to impromptu backyard parties—and the fun and sense of belonging that was associated with it. Investments in family time pay very high dividends, especially for children, who are always in search of identity and their place in the world. Make that place your family.

One good idea we put into operation when my children, Kim and Ray, were growing up, was to have a "Family Night." Everything in modern life competes for the family's after-work time. Meetings. Social engagements. If it isn't one thing, it's another. Setting aside one night a week for the family to do something together keeps the kids' sense of belonging in <u>continual</u> focus.

Find out what everyone wants to do. One Family Night activity might be to go downtown. Another might be going to the movies or out to a favorite restaurant. Or it might simply be staying at home and playing board games. Whatever it is, don't let anything interfere with it. Make Family Night sacred. Inviolable.

The specific day for Family Night may have to vary from week to week. It depends on family schedules, the kids' sports activities, or a parent's out-of-town business travel. But make it a priority and be sure everyone realizes it's a priority that somehow must be accommodated. Work it out.

And when Family Night comes, keep it loose. Have fun. Enjoy each other. More love and understanding and family solidarity can come together in Family Nights than in years of stressed-out average nights.

<u>Listening</u> to your kids is critical. A few years ago, I was in an audience-participation meeting with about 2,000 teenagers. My kids, Ray and Kim, were in the audience. At the end of the meeting, I was busy signing autographs and having my picture taken, and I was waiting for my kids to tell me how awesome I was.

Well, they didn't say anything. And when we got into the car to drive home they still didn't say anything. Five minutes went by and still nothing. So I told myself I'd give it two more miles and if they didn't say something, I'd ask them what they thought. The two miles went by and I said, *"Hey, you guys, how'd you like the meeting?"*

Kim was the outspoken one in our family and she said, *"Dad, I thought it stunk."*

"What?"

"I thought it stunk. You listen to those kids, but you never listen to Ray or me."

"What in the world are you talking about?" I asked. *"I listen to you guys all the time!"*

"No, daddy, you don't," she said.

I said, *"Compared to my father, I listen to everything you and Ray say."*

"We don't have your father," said Kim. *"You don't listen to us. You tell us. You don't have time to listen. You just tell. Anybody else, you listen to."*

It was a lesson I never forgot. Kim was right. Most of my kids' questions and problems seemed so minor compared to my own that I was in the habit of barely listening to them and just coming up with offhanded, half-attentive responses. They thought of it as lack of respect—as if their thoughts weren't important enough for me to focus on. It was my mistake—and I've done my best not to repeat it. I've always had tremendous love and respect for my kids, but I hadn't been demonstrating it. I had to clearly show them that if they thought something was important, then it was important to me.

I realized that if I didn't do that, I'd start to become less and less important to them.

In our household we created a "Trust Bank" for the kids. The object was to teach them responsibility, and it worked this way:

When they cleaned their room, came home from school on time, did their homework and chores and the other things they were supposed to do, what they were really doing was making deposits into the Trust Bank. On the other hand, if they hadn't done those things— for example, if yesterday one of them had come home from school an hour late—that was a major withdrawal from the Trust Bank.

When Ray or Kim would come to me and tell me about something they really wanted to do—such as going to a friend's party—and if it seemed okay to me—I'd say, *"Okay, I really want you to be able to do that, but let's see what's in the Trust Bank."*

Let's suppose it was Kim and she'd been the one who'd come home late from school the previous day. *"Gee, honey,"* I'd say, *"I really want you to go to that party, but yesterday you came home a whole hour later than you were supposed to and that was a big withdrawal from the Trust Bank. No matter how much I want you to go to that party and have a great time— and believe me, I really <u>want</u> you to do that—there just isn't enough in your Trust Account right now. Honey, there'll be more parties. Check with me next time—after you've made a few more deposits into your account."*

That Trust Bank idea was very successful. Anytime chores and other duties weren't done, all I'd have to say was, *"Hey, don't forget the Trust Bank."* I didn't have to say, *"Kim, go clean your room."* Or *"Ray, pick up your clothes."* Just the mention of the Trust Bank was enough. It was a positive and creative way of teaching responsibility—a way that was fair and that reinforced the children's understanding of the need for trust within the family. You can't overestimate the benefits accruing to parents and children who trust each other.

In every area of discipline, the key factor should be fairness and trust between parent and child. Punishment, for example, shouldn't be handed out at the whim of the parent. It has to be well thought out and executed.

My wife and I found it best to work out a set of punishment expectations <u>with</u> the kids—harsh, medium, and mild—so that they knew what to expect when they'd done something wrong. When Kim or Ray did something deserving of punishment, we'd discuss the punishment options and come to an agreement on it. It's amazing how straight kids can be when their honesty and fairness are directly challenged. If they think the punishment should be harsh, chances are they'll say so. They'll actually work <u>with</u> you to understand the relative seriousness of their "crime" and the punishment they deserve.

It's in that sort of mutually fair and trusting atmosphere—even where it concerns discipline—that parent-child understanding, real empathy, and good relationships are cemented for life.

It's very important for me to add that there was never a time—after punishing Ray or Kim—that my wife and I didn't process it with them. Even though they'd understood the fairness of the punishment, we'd still go over the whole matter again and reassure them that their punishment didn't mean that we didn't love them or that they were to fear Daddy or Mommy.

In our home, then, the bottom line in parent-child relationships was to give the kids an equal say in the disciplinary process so that there was a clear understanding of its need and fairness. There were no mysteries. No misunderstandings. No resentments. No feelings of unfairness. And—above all—no feelings that their parents didn't love them.

Accomplish that, and you've got a great system going with your kids. They're not likely to get that kind of treatment anywhere else. It goes a long, long way toward building family respect, love, and real togetherness.

You see, *what you're really doing is taking the time to look at the situation through your kids' knothole.* (Remember the knothole experiment I talked about earlier?) Just as you sometimes need to understand and address another adult's viewpoint to get help in achieving your mission in life, so you need to understand and address your kids' viewpoints if you expect them to help you achieve your objective of having a close-knit family.

However, even with that in mind, and despite the best of intentions, parents can sometimes be unthinking and oblivious to a kid's viewpoint. When that happens, unpleasant confrontations can arise, sometimes with long-lasting resentments. To avoid this, Zoraida and the kids and I would occasionally devise new communications language—a simple word or phrase that would immediately clue us in to the other person's feelings.

The word *"Bananas!" is* a case in point. Here's how it came about:

When Kim and Ray were growing up, I was fortunate enough to be able to provide them with a beautiful home and an indoor swimming pool. Never in my own youth had I ever had such great luxuries, and I remember kidding around with Kim one day and pushing her into the pool.

Well, I hadn't noticed that she'd just had her hair all prettied up—something she'd worked on for hours—

and when she came out of that pool she was not a happy young lady! Loudly and somewhat angrily, she said, *"Daddy, I've just done my hair!"* I took it lightly, continuing to tease her and calling her attention to the luxury of having an indoor pool. A little wet hair seemed unimportant—to me—but on this occasion it was very important <u>to her</u>!

When I finally got the message, of course I apologized. But by initially being oblivious to her viewpoint I had unwittingly engineered an unnecessary confrontation and caused hurt and resentment. Those are the last things any parent wants to inflict on a child. If it occurs often enough, the long-term effects on family unity can be disastrous.

Because we all understood what had happened, we sat down and talked about it and came up with the word *"Bananas!"* as a communications tool. We decided that from that day forward, whenever someone emphatically used this word in our house it was a signal that they were seriously offended and upset—it was not a situation to kid about and the other person was to accept that fact and back off.

It worked beautifully. *"Bananas!"* became the one-word communication that said it all. It kept the peace. It allowed an "injured" party to vent off steam and make his or her viewpoint absolutely clear. It replaced all the harsh words that might have been said when someone was upset—words which everyone involved might have later regretted. It headed off long-lasting hurt and resentment. In sum, *"Bananas!"* became one of the most important words in the Pelletier family—and it still is.

Earlier, we talked about pursuing your life's mission. To do that most successfully, you need family understanding, agreement, and togetherness on the project, and that involves your kids. They should be brought in right from the beginning—they should be made to feel a part of your mission—but there are some things to be aware of.

First of all, your dream can scare kids. It represents the unknown. It represents insecurity. They don't know what's going to happen. When you involve kids in your dream, you have to walk the line between over-involving them and under-involving them. You have to strike the right balance so that they understand without fear. It was a lesson I had to learn.

When I was getting my speaking business on its feet, every aspect of it was shared with my kids—the good parts and the bad. They were young and I wanted them to know what was going on right from the start ... I wanted them to relate to my dream. But I made the mistake of asking them for their input on complex problems they couldn't possibly resolve for me, such as financing. In fact, the subject frightened them. If their father was having trouble with financing—and here I'm talking about multiple thousands of dollars—how could they help me solve it? It was a major dose of insecurity for them. In my zeal to open up everything to them and help them understand what was going on, I was over-involving them.

On the other hand, it's extremely important for kids to hear you process things. They have wonderful insights. They're honest. They have no ax to grind. They're eager to give you support when they're brought into your plans as a family partner. They'll sacrifice to help the family achieve its dream (because it's become their dream as well). Kids will do all this—and more.

But it's necessary to avoid giving them the responsibility for making it happen. They don't know how.

It's asking too much of them. <u>You're</u> the leader. Confident. Capable. What you need from them is their understanding and support. How much better it would have been in my case if, instead of asking them for financial advice, I had said, *"Well, kids, to make this dream happen I'll have to figure out some new ways of financing. So, it may not happen right away. But with your support we'll get there, I promise you!"*

Apart from involving your kids in your dream, it's equally important to keep your kids apprised of other significant changes that you have reason to believe might be in store for the family. In today's world of corporate downsizing and re-engineering—with job losses so threatening—change is almost inevitable, and if you see it on the horizon there's nothing wrong with a family huddle in which everyone is asked for their general ideas on what to do.

For example, when you're discussing the situation you might ask everyone to consider the following: *"Do you think Daddy should go into his own business? Or do you think he should look for another job? What do you think? Let's talk about it."*

That sort of discussion brings the family together in a mutual resolve to come up with ideas, explore all possibilities, see things through, and stick together—and, above all, it doesn't shut the kids out!

As a parent, remember that these sessions must be approached in a positive manner that assures the kids everything will be for the better. They must understand that you see a job loss as an opportunity, not a disaster. You've given yourself *permission to win* and that's what will happen—for everyone. The kids are asked to see it that way and go to bed at night with those thoughts. The hard, specific problems—which the kids don't have experience enough to help you with and which would only give them a sense of insecurity and fear—are left out of the mix. It's the leader's job to find the tough answers. The leader can explain the situation and get team support, but <u>how</u> the problems are resolved is up to him (or her).

The bottom line on this is that when problems arise, too many parents don't share their feelings and plans and the kids don't have any idea what's happening. They're afraid. They're insecure. They have no sense of belonging. It's a terrible place for a kid to be. Daddy has lost his job—and now what? Unless the parent opens up to them and treats them as partners, they're likely to misinterpret everything for the worst.

You'll notice that running through all of this discussion about relationships with kids—unconditional love and respect, spending time with them, really listening to them, bringing them into the disciplinary process, discovering their viewpoints, devising ways to head off angry confrontations—running through all of this is the common thread of bringing your kids into family discussions. They're not made to feel as if they're servants or hired hands or outsiders or too young to understand anything and take part in family decisions. Just the opposite. They are made an integral part of the family structure. They have their responsibilities and duties. They share the enjoyments. They share the winnings and the penalties. They're a part of the game. They are <u>one</u> with everyone else. They're made to feel that they're just as important, just as loved and respected, and just as necessary to the family's happiness and survival as everyone else is.

Parenting is often viewed as a lifetime activity. But it's really a <u>daily</u> activity ... <u>a January 1st activity</u>.

Every day there are new and different challenges that
have to be addressed. No family is perfect or problem-
free. Kids are kids and grown-ups are grown-ups and
there will always be differences in thinking, but everyone is entitled to equal love, respect, and empathy, and
to an environment in which differences are discussed,
explained, and ironed out to everyone's agreement.

It is in <u>that</u> arrangement that a family has the best
chance of succeeding with its children ... of keeping
them within the fold, not just physically, but in their
hearts and minds as well.

And I have to tell you that when my kids were
growing up—and I was constantly traveling—Zoraida was
the person who supplied most of those necessary ingre-
dients for our family. Much of what I've written here
about kids is what I call *pain-based wisdom*—truths I
learned the hard way and much later in life—and although Zoraida and I were subsequently divorced and
our kids faced the emotional hardships of split families,
yet, thanks to her, Ray and Kim are stable and accomplished and have weathered many storms magnificently.

To this day I have no closer friend than Zoraida—
and no man was more blessed with a wife who understood and provided for the true needs of his children
than I was.

Relationships

I believe that the biggest problem in relationships
is that people approach them with a December 31st attitude. They bring all of yesterday's baggage and priorities into a new relationship and expect the other person
to magically conform. They're seeking the ideal partner—a worthy quest—but it's rare to find two people
who think and feel alike in all matters, and countless

relationships that could have been extremely successful have foundered on the rocks of such insistent conformity.

Compatibility between two people who have different profiles, but who would obviously like to be together, is not a hard thing to achieve if the differences between them are celebrated and not viewed as an obstacle. This demands a January 1st attitude ... the recognition that positive new thinking is called for. There must be new ways of looking at things, new priorities, open-mindedness, and respect for each other's different life experiences, views, and talents.

When real efforts are made in these areas, the differences between two people can turn into a plus for the relationship. Given such positive attitudes, a classical artist and a civil engineer, for example, can do just fine together. What good does it do if the artist thinks, *"Well, I can only live with another artist"*? Or if the engineer insists on having a partner who grasps physics? That's pure December 31st thinking.

A friend of mine was talking about good marriages recently, and the most solid and happy one he knew of was between a poetess and an airline pilot. The pilot was totally non-creative, and the poetess couldn't begin to understand how an airplane functioned. Yet, my friend said that in his nearly sixty years he'd never seen a more loving and compatible relationship. They celebrated their differences! It made their lives interesting.

The world is getting smaller and more complicated and challenging—and the need for meaningful relationships that will last and can weather the immense changes around us is more and more important every day. The trouble is that too many of us aren't educated in the mechanics of an awesome relationship. We don't

know how to go about it. We look backward for answers, not forward. It's that baggage I mentioned, that
December 31st attitude. It's closed-minded. We don't
know how to communicate or pull together. We don't
know how to compromise. We can't fuse our priorities
into a common goal. We see only our differences. We're
afraid of each other.

A few years ago, I was invited to speak on the
S.S. Norway for the Walt Disney Company. The Carib-
bean cruise was called FantaSea, and it was Disney's
first attempt at a cruise. Zoraida, and I had gone ashore
for a few hours on the island of St. Thomas, and I had
returned on one of the ship's tenders about an hour and
a half before she did.

During those ninety minutes, the weather had suddenly turned very stormy—the forerunner of a hurricane
that had been predicted for much later. In other words,
it caught everyone by surprise. The seas rose, the wind
picked up to gale force, and as the tenders hurriedly ferried
people back to the ship it became incredibly difficult and
dangerous to offload the passengers from the tenders
bobbing up and down in the swells.

I remember being told that some seventy or more
nationalities were represented among the crew—people
from all over the world, speaking different languages,
seemingly having little in common—yet, in a matter of
minutes the crisis had fused all of us together. Passengers and crew were forming human chains, risking their
own lives to help offload the passengers. We all had a
common purpose that was far more important than our
differences, and as one of the people in that human
chain I can tell you that never in my life have I witnessed a more positive display of diversified people
uniting to achieve a common goal.

So desperate was the situation, in fact, that 120 passengers had to be left on the island (we retrieved them later) to allow the ship to temporarily head out to sea, where it could better weather the storm. But before we left, Zoraida had been brought aboard, and I'll never forget the relief I felt when I saw she had been rescued. I cried unashamedly.

The crew and passengers on that ship could have concentrated on their differences instead of pulling together. But they didn't. For a grand moment in time, their differences, prejudices, suspicions, fears—all of their December 31st baggage—was thrown away as they came together in common purpose as a true team.

The same principles apply in a relationship.

We need to pull together. We need to collaborate. We need to be positive. We need to seek the common goals desired by both parties and focus on them through the distractions caused by our differences, doubts, and fears. We need to communicate without hurting each other. We need to acknowledge each other's feelings, compromising where necessary and thinking about everything with the end in mind.

Numberless relationships have failed to bloom because one or both parties are so mired in the past—so insistent on the other person fitting a prescribed pattern—that they're blind to the wonderful prospects of diversity. It's not stretching it to ask you to remember Branch Rickey, the Dodgers' manager who made Jackie Robinson the first black player in Major League Baseball. *That was positive January 1st thinking at its purest!* Talk about new beginnings! <u>Think</u> what those two men had to go through to accomplish a common goal! Think of the December 31st baggage <u>they</u> had to set aside!

And the result? By far the most important and positive development in American sports in the past hundred years!

In personal relationships, I admit that differences between two people can sometimes be so great that compatibility really just isn't in the cards. The relationship is neither practical nor desirable. Let's face it—it happens. But what I'm saying here is that in many cases it's really not the differences that cause a relationship to come apart—*it's the negative attitude the partners take toward those differences.* They don't know how to deal with things positively. They see only the bad, not the good.

As a winner, you won't do that. You're coaching yourself into positive approaches toward relationships and everything else in the Circle of Life. If your relationship is in trouble—or if you doubt the workability of a prospective new relationship with someone you otherwise care deeply about—your self-coaching priority is to see to it that in no way are you causing these problems by succumbing to negativity and by focusing on your December 31st baggage. It's not fair to you, and it's not fair to the other person.

I believe you must open your mind, learn to celebrate the differences, see the good, and find the common ground.

Wendy Bell is the songwriting daughter of a friend of mine who composed this line for one of the loveliest of her works: *"Roses are green—when you look beneath the blossoms."*

It's true. But nobody notices. 90% of the rose is green, and it's where the strength and beauty of the flower is developed. It's the same thing with a relationship—the sources that give it strength and beauty are often overlooked.

Look for those sources. I know you'll do that. Now is the time. It's January 1st. It's a new beginning for your relationships and for the promises they can hold.

9

WINNING IN THE WORKPLACE

When you woke up this morning it was January 1st. Ahead of you, for just this first day alone, lay a precious 86,400 seconds—a God-given gift to you to use as you wish.

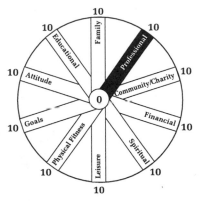

You can waste those 86,400 seconds thinking about yesterday, December 31st.

Or you can invest them in today, January 1st.

You can go forward this day with the attitude of a champion—intent on winning the game. Or you can go backward and smother yourself in doubt, uncertainty, and self-pity—and lose the game before you start.

You can <u>decide</u> to be successful today. You can plan for it. Or you don't have to decide anything. Remember, <u>not</u> *to decide is to decide!*

How this day starts, progresses, and ends is up to you. It's not up to your boss. It's not up to fate and circumstance. *It's up to the champion within you.* No matter what happens in the 86,400 seconds bestowed upon you this day, you have given yourself *permission to win*, and one way or the other I believe that your spirit and your attitude will accommodate whatever occurs, and that you will emerge as a winner at the end of the day.

If you're fired from your job, you have permission to see it as the opening up of exciting new opportunities. If you make a serious mistake in your work, I believe you will treat it as a positive learning experience rather than a disaster. If you have communication problems with bosses or co-workers, I believe you'll set your mind to resolving them rather than harboring grudges or resentments. If you're refused a raise, I believe you will concentrate on ways to make yourself so valuable to the company that they can't refuse you in the future.

At the end of this day's 86,400 seconds—regardless of what happens in your workplace—I believe you will have turned every negative into a positive. You will have turned it into an advantage that's destined to move you forward. In short, you will emerge as a winner—scarred and bruised from the game, perhaps, and maybe short of your goal, but with your positive champion's attitude fully intact and with no doubt at all about the eventual outcome.

And the next day is January 1st all over again—with another gift of 86,400 seconds in which to improve your championship form and your game plan for success.

Now, how do you plan for success?

Well, for one thing, you can get out your calendar or daily planner and headline each day's page with a motivational reminder to keep you focused. Here are some of the reminders I've written in my own daily planner: *Today's the day! ... No more excuses! ... Today I have the winning edge! ... Play like a champion! ... Knowledge is power!*

I'm sure you've heard many motivational lines that appeal to you. Write one down for every day of the month.

It's simple, but effective. Don't be like millions of other people who get up every morning and consult a blank calendar page, or one filled with uninspiring notes. That's no way to start the day. Inspire yourself! Start right out by reminding yourself you're a champion!

My all-time favorite phrase is this one: *Ain't it great!* And there's a story behind it:

A few years ago, I was in Tampa, Florida waiting for a flight. I had a few extra minutes, so I went to the Bargain Shop for a shoe-shine. There were two people shining shoes. One was an older gentleman with a ponytail and the other was a large African-American woman who had one of the most positive attitudes I had ever witnessed. She was really <u>into</u> shining shoes! She was excited about it. She was enthusiastic. She was smiling from ear to ear, tossing out quips left and right, and she was just full of warm, wonderful personality. It was infectious, it was fun, and just watching her made me feel good all over. I was hoping that when my turn came I'd get her chair and, sure enough, that's just what happened.

As soon as I sat down, she noticed a pin I had on my lapel and she asked what it was.

"That's an eagle," I said.

"Oh, I <u>love</u> eagles!" she replied. *"Why do you have one on your lapel?"*

"It's my company logo," I explained, and then I broke down the word "EAGLE" for her. *"The 'E' is for enthusiasm. 'A' is for attitude. The 'G' stands for goals. 'L' is for love. And the last 'E' stands for effort."*

Well, when she heard that, her eyes widened and she grinned from ear to ear and shouted, "AIN'T IT GREAT!" It was the way she said it that got to me. It was full of pep, like she was cheerleading. It was super-enthusiastic—the most positive thing you could ask for. *"Wow!"* I thought to myself. *"What a fantastic attitude!"*

So, we got to talking. Her name was Mrs. Cole, and bit by bit, as she shined my shoes, she told me her story.

"When I was little," she said, *"I was the daughter of a sharecropper, and I always dreamed that when I grew up I'd live in a small, beautiful white house with a white picket fence and black shutters. You know what? Today, I live in a small, beautiful white house with a white picket fence and black shutters! Ain't it great!"*

Her face was beaming, and she was so excited I couldn't hold back. *"AIN'T IT GREAT!"* I shouted back at her. *"AIN'T IT GREAT!"*

And then she laughed and said, *"You know, when I go home to my kids and say 'Kids! Ain't it great!' they say to me, 'These days, mother, we say '<u>isn't</u> it great!' "* Then she paused and looked up at me with a twinkle in her eye and said, *"AIN'T IT GREAT!"*

Friends, I have to tell you, on that day I was on my way to make a presentation to an insurance audience and I was being paid big bucks to be positive and spirited and enthusiastic. Yet here I was in the company of a person who was taking the dirt off of my shoes and who had the most positive and enthusiastic attitude I'd ever encountered. She perfectly demonstrated the winner's spirit that I coach—that no matter what, it <u>is</u> great! This is the champion's way of approaching every day of life and everything that happens. And this wonderful lady had it all!

Today, Mrs. Cole is a dear friend, and I often make it a point to see her when I go to Tampa. I've told Mrs. Cole's story many times to many audiences, and it's made a difference not only in their lives, but also in mine.

Once, when I was speaking to an audience at the Sheraton-Grand Hotel in Tampa, I arranged to have Mrs. Cole sit in the audience. Nobody knew she was there. When I finished telling her story, having many times referred to her as one of my all-time heroes, I suddenly asked her to stand up and I introduced her to the audience. Never, not in any other of my talks, have I heard such thunderous applause!

You see, there wasn't anyone in that room who didn't fully understand what that lady personified—the absolute power of a winning attitude over lifelong obstacles. She had the very thing that everyone in that room was struggling to achieve for themselves. Even to this day, people in Tampa come up to me and say, *"Hey, Ray, how's the ain't-it-great lady?"*

Just recently, the Pelletier Group (my company) gathered at the Sheraton-Grand for a retreat, and Mrs. Cole was our honored guest for luncheon. Everyone on my team, including the new members, got to meet my hero, my friend, and a real teddy bear.

So, write it down at the top of one of your calendar pages: **Ain't it great**! If there's a better motivational message to start off your day, I don't know what it is.

Always remember, you're responsible for your own career—and *attitude is everything!* I often illustrate this in my seminars by asking the audience to help me solve a problem. This is what I tell them: *"Look, I've just bought out the company, and what I want to do is make you the Senior Vice President and give you tons of money. But I need you to tell me what I should look for in the person who will replace you."*

Invariably, they start shouting answers at me. *"In-tegrity!"* shouts someone. *"A sense of humor,"* says another. *"Understanding!" "Friendliness!" "Concern!" "Confidence!"* And so on—until there are twenty or thirty different items—all the qualities they feel are essential to fulfilling their own jobs.

"Okay," I say, *"now help me process your answers."* Then I take each answer they've given me and ask them if it represents a skill or an attitude. Everybody gets into the debate and dozens of people discuss it back and forth until there's general agreement on the answer. Yes, that's a skill. No, that's an attitude. And so forth, until all the qualities have been judged.

It's amazing. Every time I've done this, and it doesn't matter what the industry is, everyone agrees that only two or three qualities on the list are skills—all the rest are <u>attitudes.</u> And all of a sudden the whole audience gets the point! I can see the "Ah-ha!" written all over their faces. By their own words, they've learned that the most important thing any of us can bring to work is our positive attitude. Attitude is <u>everything</u>!

This morning, before starting my workday, I listened to a motivational tape on the craft of speaking. In other words, at the very beginning of my day I was inputting positive information, feeding my winner's attitude, and sharpening my ax for the day's challenges that lay ahead.

I try to stay away from radio talk shows that will program me negatively. I don't want more than several minutes of news. I don't want to start my day by being bummed out and influenced by every negative news bite that's designed to grab listeners. That's no way for me— or you—to keep a champion's edge.

You need to focus on the positive and program your own inner computer with information and motivation that will enable you to leave for work with a winner's attitude. You have to give yourself a mental breakfast of positive input and confidence. You have to concentrate on the success you know you'll achieve today. *Expect a miracle to happen today!* Expect it! In fact, you should try doing what I do—I often leave the house, even on a cloudy day, wearing sunglasses. Why? To remind myself of how bright the future is! That's the positive attitude I instill in myself.

If I use props like sunglasses to remind me to stay positive, so what? It works. Sometimes I'll wear a rubber band around my wrist. If I have a negative thought, I snap it. I often suggest to my audiences that they should occasionally put a Band-Aid on the back of their right hand with the number **96** written on it. Why? Because psychologists tell us that 96% of the time we think about ourselves. True champions take their eyes off themselves to learn what other people think and feel—it gives them a better chance to influence others. It's the winner's edge.

Like everyone else, when I leave home in the morning I have concerns and worries that aren't related to my work—*but I try my hardest to leave them at home.* When I step out of that door, I'm free of the baggage that might hold me back from concentrating on success in my career.

Recently, I held a two-day seminar. During those two days, I had a pile of luggage sitting on the stage. I didn't refer to it until the end of the second day and, of course, people wondered what the luggage was all about. (I use lots of props in my meetings—ladders, chairs, even toilets—anything that will help me illustrate my points, and my meeting rooms are fun places to be. Nobody knows what's going to happen and there's an air of excitement about it.)

Finally, the time came to refer to the luggage—usually about eight suitcases—and I asked for a volunteer to come up and tell me what sort of baggage he carried home with him from work. What were the work-related problems he couldn't get off his mind when he went home? *"Well,"* he said, *"it seems I'm always facing a deadline."* So I had him pick up one of the suitcases and put it over his shoulder.

"Okay," I said, *"give me another work problem you take home with you."*

"I'm worried about the future of the company," he said. *"I don't know if I'll still have a job next year."*

I had him pick up another suitcase.

This scenario went on for a minute or so until he had come up with eight work problems and was struggling to hold eight suitcases—each suitcase representing part of the baggage he carried home with him at night. Then I had him carry the suitcases to the meeting-room door and stop. *"Alright,"* I said, *"that's the door to your house. Now what do you usually do with the baggage?"*

"Well, I bring it into the house."

At this point I had him open the door, and there on the floor were eight more suitcases. *"These are the problems you have at home,"* I told him. *"Tell me which ones you carry to work with you."* So he started to tell me, and he had to pick up a suitcase for each problem he takes to work with him. This is in addition to the eight suitcases he's already carrying, and soon he was trying to manipulate nine, then ten, and up to sixteen suitcases. Well, it's impossible—and the audience

laughed uproariously at his struggles. But everybody got the point loud and clear.

In real life, it's no laughing matter. We load ourselves down with so much baggage that we can't handle it. We bring our work problems home and our home problems to work. The load is so unmanageable we begin to think of ourselves as failures. We can't concentrate. We lose confidence. We lose faith in ourselves. We can't take any more.

Unfortunately, that's the way millions of people face their day—loaded down with baggage. This is the way they walk out of the house in the morning. This is the way they walk back into the house in the evening. Their constant attitude is one of doubt, fear, and confusion. They're overwhelmed with their problems. They're convinced that they can't find time or room in their day to attend to all their troubles. That's negative thinking, and it's nonsense.

To illustrate this in my seminars, I often fill a bowl with marbles. I jam them in, fill the bowl to the brim. Then I ask someone to verify that the bowl is filled. I ask them if there's any more room left in the bowl. They'll say, *"No. There's no way can you get anything else in that bowl."*

Then I take a box of salt and pour it into the bowl. The salt seeps down through the marbles, and in a few moments I've emptied the entire box into the bowl. Now I'll ask the volunteer again, *"Is it really full this time?"*

The volunteer will inspect it carefully, looking at it and poking a finger into it until he or she is absolutely positive there isn't a bit of room left in the bowl. *"Okay, this time it's full,"* the volunteer says.

"Are you really, really sure?" I ask.

And the volunteer will say something like, *"Oh, yeah. It's full this time. You can't get any more in there. It's full!"*

Then I empty a pitcher of water into the bowl. Instantly, everyone in the audience sees that the bowl wasn't anywhere near being full. Nowhere close to it. Of all the props, tricks, and magic I use in my seminars—and I use them all the time—I think the bowl of marbles is the biggest eye-opener.

When I do this in front of an audience—when I first show them the bowl of marbles—I explain that the bowl represents their day … the 86,400 seconds they've been given. They may think their day is full. They may think they have so much to do, so much to worry about at home and at work, that there's just no room left to get it all done. They're convinced of it.

Then I add the salt. And I tell them that if they handle the demands on their time properly, there's a lot more room in their day than they think they have. It's how they handle these demands that matters. How they prioritize them and fit them in. Maybe the marbles represent demands at work and the salt represents demands at home and in their communities. But, look, they can accommodate all of it. They can fit both the marbles and the salt into their day. There's plenty of room.

Then I add the water. The water represents time for leisure, spiritual matters, and physical fitness. And the audience is amazed! There's still plenty of room!

You see, what you can fit into your day is a matter of attitude—of deliberately arranging your mental time to make room for all things in their proper place. Remember the "A," "B," and "C" priorities I mentioned earlier? You must set your "A" priorities. You have to decide to con-

centrate on what's important. You have to be disciplined. To be a champion at work, you have to leave your domestic baggage at home. And to be a champion at home, you have to leave your business baggage at work.

It's more than just being better organized. It's a matter of our winner's <u>will</u> to do it—our will to motivate ourselves in the morning for success at work. Our will to motivate ourselves when we leave work for success at home and in our personal lives.

It's the champion's way. And you're a champion! Every challenge warrants your undivided attention—but only in its own special time and place. Even the greatest champion can't play two games at the same time. But when you play each game separately you can bring your winner's attitude fully to bear on it—and win!

Let's wrap it all up in a word—**F-A-M-E**:

F: Your day is never <u>full.</u>

A: You have the mental space to <u>accommodate</u> whatever needs to be done. Every problem and concern at work and in your personal life is an opportunity to win—an opportunity you have time to address.

M: The way you <u>manage</u> it is by prioritizing one opportunity at a time, concentrating on the issue at the proper moments in your day and motivating yourself.

E: Give it your best <u>effort</u>—all you've got! Be disciplined. Get focused, stay focused, and go for it!

It's all attitude. Attitude really <u>is</u> everything! And it takes over the moment you get out of bed in the morning and start treating yourself like the champion you are.

AIN'T IT GREAT!

Nothing can stop the man with the right mental attitude from achieving his goal; nothing on earth can help the man with the wrong mental attitude.

— Thomas Jefferson, third President of the United States

Okay, you've decided to motivate yourself in the morning and leave your domestic baggage at home. You've got the right attitude. You're focused on your workday. Now, how do you <u>stay</u> focused as different fears, problems, and doubts distract you during the day? How do you maintain your winner's edge at work and concentrate on the things that will move you forward in your career? You don't want to wallow in excuses. NO MORE EXCUSES! You want results. How do you stay focused?

It's knowing what to focus on. Most people have what I call a "wide" focus. It isn't specific enough. They're not focusing down on the things that are necessary to assure success.

In my seminars, I sometimes bring a softball into the room and ask if there's someone in the audience who's never been able to catch very well. Maybe as a kid they were terrible at it and still are. Well, a few hands go up, so I pick out a volunteer and have him or her come up to the stage. I tell them I'm going to throw them the ball and I want them to concentrate on it—but not just on the ball. I want them to focus down on the spin of the ball by watching the <u>lacings</u>.

Then I throw them the ball—and they catch it.

I keep on throwing the ball to them. They catch it every time. I bounce it off the wall, and then the floor, and maybe even the ceiling—and they still catch it! They're not surprised anymore. They're <u>amazed</u>!

Why are they able to catch it? Because they're focusing down and concentrating on the right things—the spin, the lacings. This enables them to follow the path of the ball, and they're so focused on it that when the ball gets to them they catch it automatically.

It's the same in life. Focusing on your goal, like focusing on the ball, is not enough. To assure success, it's important to focus down on the specific things that will help you attain that goal. You have to know what those things are. In your job, maybe you have to improve your communications skills. Maybe you need to take some specialized learning courses. Maybe it's important to make a friend of a person who doesn't like you. These are your "lacings." By concentrating on them, you have a better chance of realizing your goal.

As a coach, I can tell you that when you focus down on the lacings, you don't have time for fear or doubt or lack of confidence. Your whole concentration is right where it belongs—on the things that will enable you to succeed. You won't need excuses.

Let's talk about excuses. *Excuses are the loser's tools.* They're negative. They're a cop-out. They keep you from facing a problem and fixing it. They keep you from learning and progressing. You don't have any use for excuses. As you'll find me repeating many times in this book—because I mean it—*"You're better than that."* Excuses have to be buried and spit on—and here's a case where I had a bunch of people do literally that.

About two years ago, I was very honored by Phil Niekro. Phil is a former Major League Baseball pitcher and he's famous for his knuckle ball. He's a future Hall of Famer, he's been a friend of mine for many years, and on the occasion I'm referring to he'd just been given the opportunity to manage the Colorado Silver Bullets.

The Silver Bullets was the first women's professional baseball team to be officially recognized by the

---

Catching the football is all mental. You can put all the stickum on your hands you want, but what it really comes down to is pure concentration.

— John Jefferson, NFL wide receiver

National Association of Professional Baseball Leagues, and Phil had asked me to help motivate the team during their first spring training in March of 1994. This I did for some eight weeks.

1300 women from all over the country had tried out for the team, but only 55 had qualified for spring training. Yet, even among these 55 I could sense some hesitancy and fear about playing professional baseball. This could affect their performance on the field, so to get to the bottom of it—before we started training—I met with the whole group and asked them to talk with me and tell me what was on their minds.

Well, there was a lot on their minds! First of all, most of them were afraid of baseball. You see, all of them had played softball for years—but not baseball. They were comfortable with softball. They were familiar with it. They knew how it worked. All their instincts were geared to the special feel, speeds, and idiosyncrasies of softball. But now they were making a major change. It was a new world to them, and they were unsure of themselves.

Added to this was that many of the young ladies were afraid of the prejudice they might encounter. All of the instructors and coaches on the training field were men with years and years of Major League Baseball experience behind them. They personified a man's game in a man's world, and as one of the Silver Bullets said to me, *"You know what I'm afraid of? I'll tell you what I'm afraid of. I'm afraid of going onto the field with a man who's throwing a baseball 95 miles an hour at my head because he doesn't want me on the field! He doesn't want me to have the chance to compete with him in professional baseball."*

And there were other fears. In softball, for instance, these women had played with aluminum bats. Now they had to switch to wooden bats. They'd never used wooden bats. Would they be as good with wooden bats? Could they adjust? They were afraid of the change.

One by one they listed their fears, and as I listened to them I realized that what I was really hearing was excuses. They were comfortable with softball. They didn't want to change. So they came up with excuses: *"I'm not used to baseball." "How can I do well?" "I'm afraid of male players." "I don't know if I can switch to wooden bats." "Men won't accept women players."* Each one of them had worked out a specific reason that would excuse them from being top-flight players in professional baseball—and right away I understood the coaching job I had to do.

For many years, each of these women had shared the "impossible dream" of becoming professional baseball players. This is what they had hoped for and worked for so hard—and now they'd made it. They were here, a chosen few, and what I had to do was help them get beyond their excuses so they could perform at their best and prove to the world that women could bring new excitement and tremendous talent to professional baseball.

I wish you could have been there with the Silver Bullets and me at Tinker Field in Orlando, Florida. On the second day of training, there were all kinds of media in attendance—*USA Today*, ABC, CBS, *Sports Illustrated*, and everyone else you can think of—in fact, even I was wired up so I could give television reports.

After practice was over that day, I had the team walk off the field with me to another field just outside of the Citrus Bowl. Earlier that day, I'd had the groundskeeper dig a grave in the field, and after I'd positioned the team in a semicircle around the grave I asked for three women to volunteer to be pallbearers. I handed them a brand new softball and explained that they needed to put the game of softball behind them; they needed to get beyond it; they needed to put the softball in the grave and bury it forever.

But before I went any further I asked them why they loved softball so much. And one of the women answered, speaking for most of the group: *"Coach, what you don't know is that softball has been our college education. It's been our ticket to travel around the world. It's done everything for us that we couldn't afford to do for ourselves. We love softball, coach. It's meant everything in the world to us."*

And then some of them started to get teary. They knew it was over, that they had to say goodbye to something that had been a good friend to them. It was only a softball, mind you, but there are few times when I have been as deeply touched as I was when I saw the tears at that "gravesite" as they placed the softball into the grave. This was a serious and significant loss—more so than I had imagined when I had planned the "burial."

I then had three other team members place an aluminum bat into the grave. When that was done, each player and each coach took a shovelful of dirt and filled in the grave. And then an amazing thing happened. Michele McAnany, a little peanut of a player standing five-foot-one, spat into the grave after shoveling in the dirt. So determined was she to put the past behind her and bury her excuses that she sealed her resolve in front of everybody by letting go with a big wad of spit!

Immediately, the trance of sadness was broken. Michele had turned December 31st into January 1st right on the spot! Yesterday was gone. Softball was over. Now let's get on with <u>baseball</u>! I'll never forget that little lady. It was sheer magic!

Later, in the clubhouse, I asked them one by one to go over their excuses, to relist them for me. They obliged, and after they finished I told them that at the count of three I wanted every one of them to spit on their excuses like Michele had done. Fortunately for the clubhouse custodian, their mouths were dry, but they went through the motion and the deed was done.

Softball was now truly over. Their eyes sparkled, good-humored cracks were made—and I could tell from many years of experience that every Silver Bullet in that room was now ready and eager to play <u>baseball</u>— to challenge the men on a professional level and play their hearts out.

I'm asking each and every one of you reading this to do what Michele did. Bury your excuses and spit on them!

As I often say to my seminar audiences, don't you dare tell me what you lack. Tell me what you've got! Don't you dare be negative. Be <u>positive</u>! Don't you dare be afraid. Rise above it! Be determined! Treat fears, doubts, and lack of confidence for what they are—<u>excuses</u>! Don't have anything to do with them. They all disappear when you give yourself *permission to win*— when you acknowledge the champion inside yourself!

A champion faces fear and overcomes it. A champion trains, learns, self-motivates, and does whatever it takes to replace doubt and uncertainty with confidence. Don't you dare tell me you can't make it because you don't have the best education or because you're a member of a minority or because you don't have enough time or enough money or enough help or enough anything else. NO MORE EXCUSES!

When you motivate yourself the moment you get up in the morning, you're arming yourself with the big weapon against negativity—against the fears, the doubts, the excuses that will crop up during the day. (I know a man in a 12-step program. He works hard at his sobriety, and before his feet hit the floor in the morning he gets on his knees and prays: *"God, I need your will in my life. I don't want to drink, do drugs, or smoke today. Thy will be done—not mine."*)

Identify and <u>focus down</u> on the challenges that will help you get where you want to go. Take <u>one challenge</u> at a time so you can deal with it effectively. There's nothing mysterious about any of this. It's not difficult. It's all attitude. The only enemy you have is negativity.

Zig Ziglar tells a great story about the training of fleas for flea circuses. They put a baby flea in a medicine bottle and cap the bottle. The flea's natural instinct is to jump—like our natural instinct is to get ahead. Well, the little flea jumps, hits the lid and says, *"Boy! that hurts!"* After a couple of days of trying this and getting a few bumps on his head, the flea knows just how high he can jump—just shy of the top of the bottle—without getting hurt. The flea trainer then takes the flea out of the bottle and puts him on the table—and for the rest of his life the flea will only jump the height of the bottle.

Don't tell me how rocky the sea is, just bring the darn ship in.

— Lou Holtz, college football coach

There can be no excuses. You can't say that you didn't like the snow or that you didn't feel up to top form.

— Jean-Claude Killy,
skier; three-time Olympic Gold Medalist

What's <u>your</u> lid? What's <u>your</u> excuse for not jumping higher than the bottle and getting ahead? Who trained you to jump just so high and no further?

Get rid of the lid. Get rid of your excuses. *You're better than that!*

When something negative happens to you or you hear something negative about yourself, when somebody tells you something that dishonors you or takes away your power, instantly tell yourself, *"I'm better than that! I'm a whole lot better than that!"*

I recently did a meeting for Bayer in Cancun, Mexico, and a young lady came up to me and said, *"Hey, coach, I've got a great line for you. When I was in college, I had a professor who challenged me. He told me there are two kinds of people in this world—Velcro people and Teflon people."*

The college professor was right. You see, if you're Velcro, everything sticks to you—if you encounter a negative attitude, it sticks to you. But if you're Teflon, a negative attitude just rolls off. It doesn't affect you. The Teflon person says, *"I'm better than that!"*

That's the key—<u>positive</u> self-talk that helps you win!

When you motivate yourself to be a winner and go to your place of work all fired up and determined to focus down on the challenges that will move you ahead—and then somebody throws a negative curve at you or you start to have self-doubts—just remember one thing: You're Teflon. Let it roll off. *You're better than that!*

Everything I've said in this chapter really boils down to having a January 1st attitude. Today is the first day of your new life. You're motivated. You're ready. Yesterday is gone. Negativity is finished; you won't let

it affect you. You have things to do, obstacles to overcome, dreams to fulfill. This is the attitude of the
champion inside you—the attitude of the winner. It's
the profound moving of the human spirit. Listen to it
and honor it. It will lift you up from narrow confines
and over barriers of grief and the ruinous fears and
doubts that everywhere seek to hold you back and limit
your achievement—and it can take you to marvelous
places of renewal, confidence, and accomplishment. Here
is where the true magic of life lies. It is within you—
wholly within you.

A few years ago, I was asked to have a talk with
a very successful businessman who was struggling with
a truly awful situation. He had been shot in the head and
left paralyzed by someone robbing his home. When I made
my first contact with him by telephone, he said that he
had been expecting my call, and then he started to cry.
I asked if he was crying because of physical pain or
emotional pain, and when he said it was emotional I knew
I'd be facing one of the most tragic challenges of my life.

This was a young man who'd had everything—he
was recognized for his business and athletic success, he
was wealthy, had a magnificent home, and he traveled
all over the world. Then, in one brief, horrible moment,
his life was completely changed.

When we finally met at his home, I'll never forget
the resignation and defeat evident in his face, his words,
and his movements. He'd given up. On the wall was a
beautiful photograph of him running on a beach. He
nodded toward it—and in that nod, the way he did it,
was expressed all the sadness and loss and awfulness
of what had happened to him.

I immediately rose from my chair, walked over to
the photograph and took it down from the wall. He had

to have <u>new</u> goals now. Running was not realistic. Focusing on that photograph—for now—was locking him into a past that had been ended by that bullet. He had a different mountain to climb, a different kind of championship ahead of him.

There are people reading this right now who believe they have been destroyed by far lesser problems—perhaps by the loss of a job in middle age and the medical coverage and pension fund that went with it. These problems might not compare with paralysis, but they are very serious and very real, and they're shared by tens of thousands in today's workplace. But just as surely as the problems are real, so is the path to victory. And that path is in the mind.

Christopher Reeve, as I'm sure you know, is famous for his movie role as Superman. After he was thrown from a horse and paralyzed—and while undergoing continuing therapy—ABC's Barbara Walters interviewed him and gave the world a precious gift. She gave us an insight into a man who was struggling mightily to rise above his paralysis with a positive attitude—and she saw to it that this experience could be shared by millions.

I often talk about Superman in my seminars—and these days I relate it to Christopher Reeve. I think all of us have wanted to be Superman or Superwoman at one time or another. We want to have our cape on and have our kids think of us as superhuman and perfect. In reality, though, there's a lot of kryptonite in our lives—things that steal our power. And what steals our power? It's a negative attitude. It's December 31st thinking.

Christopher Reeve has January 1st thinking. Has he ever heard me speak? I doubt it. Does he know the January 1st message? Probably not. But Christopher

Reeve is a professor of the January 1st message. With one of the most stirring examples of a positive attitude I have ever seen, he is overcoming the kryptonite. He may be paralyzed in his body—but he is beating it in his mind. And who's to say he won't eventually beat it in his body as well?

I expect nothing less from everyone I coach. As famous basketball coach Pat Riley once put it, *"You're either in or you're out."* And by that he was referring to his players' commitment. They were already on the team and in the game. But if they were to win it would depend upon their being in a winner's frame of mind.

The next time you leave for work, take that "in" attitude with you. You're already on the team and in the game. All you need is the winning attitude. Establishing that attitude and focusing down on your objectives are your first goals for each and every day.

In the immortal words of Johnny Air Line—one of the world's leading motorcycle stuntmen (he jumped his motorcycle over an oncoming train—<u>lengthwise</u>, not crosswise): *"If you look at obstacles, you take your eyes off your goals."* That's what he said, and that's what he did. If he can stake his life on it, so can you.

Many problems in the workplace are caused by management. Lack of employee morale and productivity, poor communications, lack of employee trust in the company ... these shortcomings are endless and pervasive in today's corporations, and the great bulk of my speaking is in response to management's growing con-

---

I am the greatest. I said that even before I knew I was. Don't tell me I can't do something. Don't tell me it's impossible. Don't tell me I'm not the greatest. I'm the double greatest.
— Muhammad Ali, professional boxer

cern with these issues. No company deliberately sets out to alienate its employees or sabotage itself, but problems caused by December 31st thinking are inbred in thousands of corporations, and correcting it provides me with a lively business. I won't address that subject in depth in this book—it requires a book of its own—but what I <u>can</u> do is coach you in some of the things to look for when you're job-hunting and planning your career. Knowing the right things to look for in a prospective employer is part of winning, and it often has little to do with the title being held out to you or the salary being offered. It has to do with the employer's <u>attitude</u>.

Of all the corporations I've worked with, it's my opinion that Viking Components, a computer memory company in Laguna Hills, California, does the most terrific job of inspiring employee trust, morale, and productivity. You'll be mesmerized when you hear what this company does for its employees. (And just as surely, some corporate executives who may be reading this book will come up with reasons why they can't do the same thing in their own company: *"We don't have enough money." "Our management would never do that."* And so on. Excuses.)

Until I'd been brought aboard as a consultant for Viking, I was positive my own company was as employee-oriented as any I'd seen. I'd had the benefit of hearing thousands of employees in other companies complain about management, so I knew how to eliminate these problems in building my own firm.

I empowered my employees, gave them freedom, communicated with them clearly, paid them well, gladly accommodated their personal and family problems, explained company goals in depth, and constantly sought their input. Most important, perhaps, I gave them permission to <u>fail</u>. New team members are especially afraid of failing, but it's in failing that you learn to be successful. Rick Pitino, head basketball coach at the University of Kentucky, has this to say about it: *"Failure is good. It's fertilizer. Everything I've learned, I've learned from making mistakes."* Well, that's how I felt about it. I didn't want my team to be afraid of risk that might lead to initial failures. I encouraged them to come up with new ideas and try out new things—not to be afraid of failure. In fact, giving them permission to fail was my way of giving them *permission to win.*

In every way, then—calling upon my own instincts and honed sense of employee relations as well as the years of input I'd had from thousands of employees in other companies—I thought I had about the best employee-oriented company in existence.

But then I came across Viking Components.

Viking is headed by Glenn McCusker, a pre-eminent entrepreneur with a very strong sales background and a great personality. At this writing, he's 34 years old. Eight years ago, he had already saved $20,000 of his own money and he had combined this with $60,000 borrowed from his parents to buy Viking Computer Products—the company he was employed by and which was on the verge of going out of business.

McCusker bought the failing company in 1987 and changed the name to Viking Components in 1988. By the end of 1995, under McCusker's leadership, Viking had 155 employees, and in that year it had $350 million in sales, an average of $2.26 million in sales for each employee! That, friends, is phenomenal! And McCusker owns 100% of the company.

As Glenn McCusker will tell you, there's no way on earth such success can be accomplished without 100% support from his team. How does he get that kind of incredible support and loyalty? What sort of magic does he weave to get so much out of so few? What makes Viking a company which, from an employee's standpoint, is to die for?

The answer is that he understands people—and I mean deeply, not superficially. He's intuitively attuned to the positive traits about people that make them uniquely promising. He's likely to hire a waitress with an attitude he admires over a technical wizard with the right skills but the wrong attitude. He can teach skills. But he can't teach attitude. It's attitude—the kind that is positive, confident, and uplifting to be around—that is his first criterion when selecting employees. Attitude speaks volumes for the prospective employee's talents, learning abilities, honesty, decency, willingness to work, ability to get along with others, and progress. Indeed, in <u>attitude</u> is found everything that goes to make up a potentially ideal employee. It clearly reveals almost every clue as to how that person will work out.

To put it a different way, Glenn McCusker *measures the real human being in his prospective team members.* I submit that there is no fairer method by which a job applicant can be judged—and that anyone treated so fairly, and then hired, will be likely to gladly and eagerly expend themselves on behalf of the company's progress and success. Is there anyone reading this—anyone at all—who wouldn't feel blessed to run into a Glenn McCusker during job searches in their particular field? Is there anyone who wouldn't immediately be inspired to give their all to the company? I doubt it.

We know what McCusker's attitude is toward you when you apply for a job, but does that attitude remain just as understanding and refreshing after you're hired? I'll tell you, but you probably won't believe it:

Bonuses are paid quarterly. If you've been on the payroll three months and the company is doing well, you get a bonus. A significant one. I heard McCusker call out to an employee during a meeting and ask him how long he'd been with the company. *"Three months,"* he said. *"How much was your bonus?"* asked McCusker. *"Eight hundred and forty dollars,"* said the employee.

Not bad for being on the job for three months! That employee will get another bonus three months later. And another three months after that. And so on.

Viking has a masseuse—on staff. Her job is to give anyone a massage when they're stressed out and need it.

Viking has an on-premises gymnasium. Aerobics instruction. Kick-boxing lessons.

Viking provides financial planning classes for everyone in the company. When they need help with budgets, bills, taxes, etc., all the professional advice is right there for the asking, any time they want it.

During the "twelve days of Christmas," McCusker buys everyone in the company a different gift for each of the twelve days. Twelve days, twelve gifts. *Substantial* gifts.

He gives Christmas parties like you wouldn't believe. He invites in entertainment groups such as Huey Lewis and the News.

During the year, at employee meetings, he'll bring in motivational speakers such as Lou Holtz, Pat Riley, and myself. That's not your run-of-the-mill meeting. It's an experience; it makes you want to get your whole family into the room. McCusker, in fact, holds the most creative meetings I've ever witnessed. I think I'm enter-taining when I speak. But McCusker will hold meetings in which everyone comes in pajamas—a pajama party! You never know what's coming next.

And his employees eat it up! They love it! I've never seen such good rapport between a company and its employees. McCusker genuinely likes his people, and out of that genuineness comes a special thoughtfulness toward them that I think is unmatched. He respects them, enjoys their company, listens and responds to them, invests in them, and helps them in unusual ways. He's a master at communicating with his people in ways that reach both their hearts and their minds. Everyone knows the job they have to do and where they stand. There are no mysteries at Viking.

Do you know that in the sixteen years I've been researching employee attitudes for my seminars, I've made it a standard practice to always ask, *"Does this company care more about people or about profits?"* In those sixteen years, <u>every</u> employee group I've consulted with—<u>except one</u>—said their company cared more about profits.

The exception was Viking Components. The answer was: *"This company cares more about people."*

Is Viking a perfect company? Absolutely not.

Is Glenn McCusker a perfect person? Absolutely not.

But do they have the right methodology? YOU BET!

McCusker understands that people do their best only for other people that they like and respect. This truth applies to <u>his</u> doing his best for his employees as well as to <u>their</u> doing their best for him. To meet the challenge of doing his best for his employees, he chooses people with attitudes and profiles he admires. Right from the start, then, he <u>likes</u> them. It's instinctive from that point to continually create thoughtful ways to show it. And show it he does! There isn't room in this book to fully list the benefits (both practical and inspirational) he bestows upon his people.

His employees, in turn, like <u>him</u>. They're passionate about the company they work for. They're motivated. They know their mission. They play to win. Because they like McCusker, they're empowered to do their very best—individually and as a team.

You know what's happening here, don't you? Both the company and the employees are treating each other as they, themselves, want to be treated This doesn't generally happen in business. In all too many companies, it's often a low-key adversarial scenario in which management-employee communication is not all it should be and creates behind-the-scenes grumbling on both sides. This breeds uneasiness and job insecurity among employees and can exact a huge cost in lost concentration, productivity, efficiency, and teamwork. There's absolutely no need for it, and the answers really aren't complicated.

Every team has a "hot" button. Management needs to discover what it is—and address it—to get the response and loyalty they want. In the end, in one form or another, it always boils down to the great wisdom of doing unto others as you would have them do unto you. It's amazing how responsive employees will be if they even <u>sense</u> that management is doing its best to do that. It isn't money a company needs to inspire its employees—it's <u>communication</u>. When Glenn McCusker started out with his $80,000, it sure wasn't money that earned him the loyalty of his team!

I hope there's a Viking in your life—or something close to it.

If you're thinking of changing jobs, you can improve your winner's edge by knowing everything you can about your prospective employer's attitude toward employees. If you can arrange it, talk with some of the employees. Get a good fix on their feelings. How enthusiastic are they? Do they <u>like</u> top management and its philosophies? Are they excited about the way they're treated? Do they know exactly what their job objectives are, or are they confused by lack of communication? Do you sense that they have a genuine and personal warmth toward the company? All of this is valuable information—more valuable for long-lasting job satisfaction than anything else you might discover about the company. More can be learned about a company from employee and management attitudes than from any company profile or balance sheet.

Now, there's something else I want you to think about. Dr. Stephen Covey, author of *The Seven Habits of Highly Effective People*, asks this question of his readers: *"Do you concentrate on the urgent or the important?"*

That one question made a significant change in my life—and if it makes you stop and think, as it did me, it can also cause a big change in your life.

Most of us concentrate on the urgent. We chase rabbits. We forget the important. We forget our mission. Someone comes up to us and says, *"Hey, I've got this opportunity for you!"* and we rush into it. It's urgent. Or maybe we're financially stressed and we see a quick answer—only it isn't an answer that furthers our mission.

What we're doing in these cases is sabotaging ourselves—I did it for years—paying far more attention to the urgent than to the important. Countless times, I was thrown off course, losing sight of my mission, in order to attend to one urgent matter after another.

A friend of mine had a 17-year-old son with an extraordinary talent for baseball. He wasn't just good—he was far, far beyond that and had the makings of a superstar. Every once in a while, a superb natural talent comes along and it's obvious to fellow players and to tough, realistic, no-nonsense coaches that they're in the company of someone truly special—one of the very few who really could be headed for the Major Leagues; the one guy out of 100,000 who could make it. This kid was like that.

The parents and coaches of this youngster urged him to get a job during the summers with the nearby Boston Red Sox doing *anything*—sweeping up, carrying water, whatever might be offered—so he could get a feeling for the Major League atmosphere and start making some important contacts. In other words, they wanted him to stay focused on professional baseball and expose him to scouts and coaches. In fact, one of his parents' friends had solid, personal contacts with Red Sox management and was certain some kind of job could be quickly arranged. It would pay next to nothing, but the exposure and learning would be fantastic.

As for the kid himself, more than anything else on earth he wanted to play professional ball. It was his dream.

But there was something else on his mind. Something more urgent. The dream could wait. He wanted a car. And I'm sorry to report that the dream indeed waited while he spent the summer doing yard work for a local contractor for wages that enabled him to get a car by summer's end.

The next summer, he took the same job again. And he did the same thing the third summer when he was on vacation from college. To make a long story short, this young man has now graduated from college, headed off into a desk job somewhere, and hasn't touched a baseball, as far as I know, since his last year in high school. His old coach—who says of this kid that he was *"the greatest natural talent I'd ever seen or worked with"*—would have given his life to promote that boy, and to this day he considers himself a failure for not having convinced the kid to take that summer job with the Red Sox.

There are urgent things in everyone's life. We've all faced situations, for example, in which we needed money immediately. The winner's method of handling it is to earn that money in a way that doesn't interfere with his or her mission. That young man, for instance— if he was really focused on his mission—could have worked for the Red Sox and then waited tables at night for extra cash.

But that's not what he did. He was <u>blinded</u> to the important by his desire to attend to the urgent. He thought he had to make a choice. In reality, if he'd stopped to think about it carefully, he could have accomplished both the urgent and the important.

As you go through life, you'll face such seeming choices again and again. But the need to make that choice is only in your mind—making a choice really isn't necessary. If you're determined to accomplish your mission—if you are wholly dedicated—I believe you'll find a way to take care of the urgent while you take care of the important. If you're committed, you'll never lose sight of your mission and its overriding importance in everything you plan and do.

One of my coach friends once said to me: *"Commitment is like a bacon-and-eggs breakfast. The chicken's involved. But the pig is committed!"*

Be committed. Your future is absolutely dependent on it.

In the summer of 1995, I was privileged to act as Master of Ceremonies for the Walt Disney Company's symposium on the future held at Disneyland Paris. The name of the symposium was "The City In 2020," and its purpose was to take a futuristic look at our society in the 21st century.

The 43 panel members came from many countries and included the finest thinkers of our age. There were technologists, architects, builders, futurists, planners, government advisers, engineers, computer specialists, social scientists—the most world-renowned people in dozens of fields and disciplines.

For example, Marvin Minsky was there, the "father" of artificial intelligence. And Georges Nahon, Director of Advanced Technology at Microsoft Europe. Bran Ferren, head of Walt Disney Imagineering, was there. David Lock was there, the Chief Planning Adviser for the United Kingdom's Department of the Environment. IBM, BT, and France Telecom were represented. And so on. It was incredible.

Here were people dealing with visions and missions. The whole subject was the future. What would it be like? How would we be living? What would we do? How would we move around? What would be the key to success? What would our society be like? It was all debated, hour after hour, for several days.

Once a man has made a commitment to a way of life, he puts the greatest strength in the world behind him. It's something we call heart power. Once a man has made this commitment, nothing will stop him short of success.
                                    — Vince Lombardi, NFL coach

You can imagine the profound "imagineering" and revolutionary ideas that graced that symposium—and all this by the world's leading stars in their fields. It was astounding to be there just to listen. Discussing manufacturing possibilities in futuristic technology, Marvin Minsky said, *"If you know what you want to create, you should be able to figure out where each atom in that product is, and place it there. If you poured the right atoms into a vat you could get a refrigerator in ten minutes at very low cost."*

Amazing stuff!

But, you know what? It was a class of elementary school children who told me what the world was really going to be like in 2020.

Just before the symposium, I asked twenty or thirty children (ages seven and eight) to make drawings of their vision for that future time. They were multilingual, and I had them come up on the stage (they were as nervous and excited as they could be) and introduce themselves. Then I had each one give their drawings to a panel member of their choice and ask that panel member to do his or her best to make the drawings come true.

It was magical! Here were the dreams of kids—their visions. And I was very excited because I know that it's from such childhood dreams that missions are born, goals are set, and visions emerge into reality. It's through such visions that society changes. We were looking at the real future. It was right there in those children's drawings. Maybe the visions portrayed would be altered and refined as the dreamers grew older and wedded the practical and attainable with the dreaming—but here was the foundation of it, the gist of it. Here was the outline of our world in 2020.

You see, I believe what I said several chapters ago: *"You have to wish upon a star ... dream like a kid again. Your potential is unlimited. You can accomplish anything you believe you can accomplish! You need the spirit and passion and heart and optimism you had when you were young enough to <u>know</u> that everything was possible. Because it really <u>is</u>!"*

Some of those kids will follow their vision. They'll accomplish their mission in life. Their visions will come true. I know it. It's the world I expect to live in.

And because <u>you've</u> given yourself *permission to win*—and because <u>you're</u> willing to dream like a kid again and accomplish your dreams—so will <u>your</u> visions come true.

Just never forget that vision. Focus on it; motivate yourself every day of your life. At work. At home. Wherever you are. Never lose sight of who you really are and what's important to you. And never, never allow yourself to be discouraged or overcome by negativity. *You're better than that!*

Hey, AIN'T IT GREAT!

The human spirit is indomitable. No one can say you must not run faster than this or jump higher than that. There will never be a time when the human spirit will not be able to better existing world marks.

— Roger Bannister,
first man to run the mile in under four minutes

10

GIVE YOURSELF AWAY

Common to all of the major religions and philosophies by which humans are encouraged to conduct their lives is the concept of helping others and thereby reaping spiritual benefits for oneself. Regardless of how you may define "spiritual," the greatest thinkers and most influential personages of history, despite varying beliefs in many areas, have all come together on that central issue. It's most memorably expressed, perhaps, by the Apostle Paul in the Book of Acts. We're all familiar with it: ***"It is more blessed to give than to*** receit."

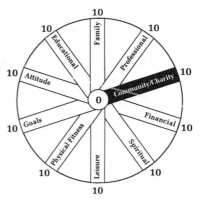

Now, why is this so? Why would these most eminent leaders of philosophy and religion—though they might debate each other to exhaustion on every other principle and belief—why would they agree on that one teaching?

Because it's a truth beyond any possible or conceivable contention, a truth common to the human experience in which millions have found fulfillment and deep measures of happiness in helping others.

As food fills our bellies and water quenches our thirst, so the giving of ourselves to others gladdens our hearts and our spirits with a sense of having done the right thing. That is the blessing—the <u>knowing</u> that we have made life a little better for someone else.

So, with the concurrence of every religion and philosophy of consequence since the dawn of history, let's start with that basic concept. And let's put it simply: <u>you cannot be truly happy and fulfilled unless you give to others</u>. It's as important to your well-being as food and water.

Now, the giving I'm talking about here is mostly the giving of your interest and time. I'm talking about love and compassion and concern, the real stuff of giving—not necessarily money.

The principal reason most people don't give of themselves—to community programs and worthy causes—is because it's not a high enough priority. There's simply too much going on in their lives—or so they think—to accommodate involvement with such things.

That's an excuse, and I don't buy it. After reading the last chapter, you know there's no such thing as not enough time or space in your day to serve others (remember the bowl of marbles). You have to <u>decide</u> to make volunteer work a priority and fit it in. It's a vital part of being a true champion—a status that can never be realized fully unless you give yourself away to those who need your help.

I challenge you to think for a minute about a cause that would interest you. You know yourself. You know about social and human conditions and situations that make you angry or upset. You know what you'd <u>like</u> to do something about. You know your talents and incli-

---

What I spent I had; what I kept I lost; what I gave I have.
— Henry Ward Bucher, English clergyman/reformer

nations and where you could be of service. You know all these things. Sort it all out and focus on just a couple of areas. You know whether you work better with young people or adults. Sort it all out.

Do you want to help get drunk drivers off the road? Do you want to help battered women? Do you want to feed the hungry, aid the homeless, be a Big Brother or Sister, take meals to shut-ins? Do you want to do what you can to help in the fight against cancer, multiple sclerosis, or any of the other countless infirmities of mankind? Do you want to preserve the environment? Help the Red Cross, Salvation Army, United Fund, or any other charity? Do you want to improve your community? Promote political objectives? Work with Little League? The list is endless; there are thousands of needs and things to do. And there are countless organizations, made up of people just like you, who would eagerly welcome your time, effort, and help.

I challenge you today to focus on a few of these causes—even one—and offer your services in some small way. And this I promise you: if you choose a cause that interests you and fits your talents and profile—in other words, something that instinctively appeals to you—I promise that you'll add new meaning to your life. You'll wonder how you ever did without it, and I speak from my own experience. Not only will it change you; it will help you be a winner. And this is why:

Whatever your life's mission may be, and whatever challenges and delays and disappointments you may encounter on your way to eventual success, no day in which you give of yourself to others will be viewed by you as negative. If everything else in your life falls apart on a given day, but you have helped someone less fortunate than yourself, that day will be viewed by you as positive.

The self-healing power of serving others is incredible. I know of no other psychological force that will more surely enable you to go to bed at night and maintain your positive champion's attitude—and this despite your own problems and disappointments. *Serving others is the quintessential winner's edge.*

It is the blessing spoken of at the beginning of this chapter—and I want you to have it.

In my files are dozens and dozens of examples of people helping other people, of people making room in their busy lives to lend a hand to the sick and the unfortunate, or to community projects. In some cases, they were moved to serve because illness or misfortune touched their own lives or the lives of family or friends, but in many other cases no such trigger was needed—they just saw the need and they pitched in to help.

You don't have to be hungry to understand what it's like for those who are hungry, or attempt suicide to understand the hopelessness of those that do. You don't have to live near a toxic dump to know how desperately environmental watchdog groups need your volunteer help and support, or be on your deathbed to understand the immense importance of hospice groups and the terminal comfort and hope they provide. You just have to care.

Hugh O'Brien, who played the role of Wyatt Earp on television for many years, cared deeply about young people, but he had no children of his own. Today, he has tens of thousands. Knowing that youngsters were often unaware of the opportunities life offered them, he started the Hugh O'Brien Youth Foundation (HOBY), a program which brings high school sophomores together in weekend leadership retreats staffed by executives and others who have achieved success in their fields. The kids are mentored in these retreats—exposed to new ideas and careers and empowered to seek accomplishment and fulfillment.

Worthy causes such as HOBY abound wherever you look, and they change society dramatically. Who's to say that the few hours volunteered by a lawyer to speak at a HOBY group on a given weekend aren't directly responsible for enlightening a youngster to such an extent that he or she eventually becomes a judge rather than a convict?

Richard Drorbaugh, a young man whose family was decimated by cancer, rode a bike around the world in 1994 to promote cancer awareness and raised $35,000 for cancer research. His recent book, *World Ride*, is an exciting account of his adventures and opens up continuing opportunities for him to speak on behalf of his cause. One person like Richard, volunteering time and effort, can indeed make a difference. And you don't have to do really big things.

Think of the good done by volunteers who answer phones for the Red Cross, or who join with others in visiting shut-ins or delivering food packages, or who help organize or promote charitable fund drives in their communities, or who give their support in other ways to causes they believe in. Imagine if nobody did these things! Imagine if nobody had the time or the interest.

But it can't happen ... because you'll be there. Let me explain:

At the very beginning of this book (the very first sentence of Chapter One), I said: *"Every audience I speak to is a championship audience."* I went on to explain that no matter who you are, that champion is in you, and I am confident you're going to bring it out and be that champion.

Now, what this means is that you are going to know what championship is. And one thing you'll come to understand—fully and with absolute clarity—is that there's no such thing as being a champion for yourself *and not for others.*

You see, as a champion your entire view of things will be positive, confident, perceptive, and action-oriented. You'll see social conditions and other problems of humankind in a new light. You will see suffering where it isn't necessary, hopelessness where there is no reason for it, failure where there can be achievement, violence where there can be peace. You'll be seeing these things through new eyes. You'll see the positive, not the negative. You'll see what <u>can</u> be done, not what <u>can't</u> be done. You will better understand, you will care. And you will act.

I don't think it, I *know* it, which is why I put it in such unqualified terms. You'll be processing things with the psyche of a champion, because that's what you are. You'll understand problem-solving as you never understood it before, and you'll be motivated to apply it to the unending miseries of the human condition which surround you everywhere you look and which you have now <u>really</u> noticed, perhaps for the first time.

So that's why I can't imagine a society in which nobody serves or cares or can't find the time to volunteer for social and charitable causes. It's impossible. <u>You'll</u> be there.

And I'll be there with you. I've never bothered to figure out the hours precisely, but a lot of my time is devoted in one way or another to a long list of worthy causes. I've chosen my projects carefully, making certain they fit my deepest interests and talents so I can contribute my time with enthusiasm and results—and this determination to serve others lies behind every word of every vision and mission statement I've ever written, both for myself and for my company. I'm sure my team will agree that it's our very reason for being.

And as we accomplish it, I can tell you it brings blessings and fulfillment beyond any ability of ours to express.

I want you to have those blessings.

Indeed I do. And you <u>will</u> have them as the champion within you emerges and you start giving yourself away.

11

FISCAL FITNESS

A few years ago, I'd have been the least qualified person on this planet to talk to you about keeping your financial matters under control. Mine were horrendous.

As I concentrated on my mission in life, there were times when I truly and literally did not know where the next dime was coming from.

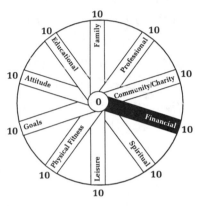

By the grace of God—and I must assign the credit to Him—my financial mess wasn't lethal and I was able to go ahead with my mission and eventually walk into the fiscal sunshine.

It was a journey-and-a-half, I can tell you, and the coaching advice I offer in this chapter is based on the lessons I've learned. It's real-life, "been there, done that," and if there's a better way to get at the facts one needs to grasp, I don't know what it is.

Because I believe you'll be dedicated to your mission, as I was, everything I say here should be 100% applicable.

I know that quite a few people reading this book are multimillionaires. You're very, very wealthy; you've already mastered this area in your life and need little coaching. The thoughts in this chapter are for those who are struggling to get on the right track and need a little more knowledge or prodding. Frankly, I don't consider that I have fully mastered this area in my own life, but I do know that if I'd paid attention to the things I'm about to say here, I would have been spared the necessity of learning it the hard way.

Many times in this book, I've urged you to concentrate on your mission and stay focused on the important rather than the urgent. Among the "important" items is managing your financial affairs properly so you can focus on your mission and not be distracted and sabotaged by continuing financial crises. Nothing will throw your mission off track faster than running out of money for the essentials—food, rent, mortgage payments, taxes, and so on. At that point, you'll have no choice but to set your mission aside and turn your full attention to financial matters—an unwelcome interruption that could put your mission on hold for weeks, months, or even years.

Several years ago, a man who has since become a close friend of mine had an extraordinary spiritual experience which immediately impelled him to forsake his career and devote himself to understanding and writing about the remarkable event which had occurred to him. The biblical research, writing, and rewriting entailed in this effort was prodigious and seemingly unending. He immersed himself in it, totally dedicating himself to his mission, and abandoned all of his commercial work except for just enough to provide a bare living.

Month after month, he literally lived hand-to-mouth; he was continually in debt and barely able to pay his rent. On several occasions, his financial condition became so desperate that he had to completely turn away from his mission for a few months and wholly concentrate on earning money.

Every time that happened, he found it extremely difficult to pick up his research where he'd left off. It was the sort of research that demanded at least a few hours of <u>daily</u> effort, this being the only way he could retain the thrust of very complex study, and when he had to leave it for a few months it would take weeks of review for him to reorient himself. Many times, in fact, he had to literally start over again from the beginning to regain his former train of thought.

As a consequence, his mission suffered, he accomplished much less than he'd hoped, and he was continually frustrated and discouraged with himself. He and I talked about it recently and I'm glad to report that he's made a decision that will help him tremendously.

He discovered what was important—and that was to split his day evenly between research and earning a sustainable income. He now understands the critical importance of attending to both on a daily basis. He will no longer allow himself to get so caught up in his research, paying so little attention to his finances, that he goes flat broke and suddenly has to abandon his mission for months at a time to pay his bills.

I know this man well. He's <u>decided</u> to do this and has given himself permission. That means he'll do it, and that his mission <u>and</u> his financial health will progress far faster than they did before.

There's a lesson in my friend's story that applies to all of us. As you may remember from my chapter on goals and missions, we first determine our mission in life, then we determine the goals we have to fulfill in order to achieve that mission. We've seen that one of the most important goals to fulfill—no matter what your mission may be—is keeping your finances in order.

As my friend learned the hard way, *he couldn't pursue his mission properly without maintaining the financial ability to do so.* Both his mission and his finances had to be attended to at the same time.

That's the lesson we all need to learn—and I had to learn it in real life just as my friend did.

I know from experience how completely a mission can take you over—you're likely to have no thought for anything else. But when it comes to finances, lack of attention is a huge strategic mistake that can lead you into one financial crisis after another and rob you of real progress in achieving your mission.

Face it: you <u>need</u> money to function—and I'm not talking about propping yourself up with millions of dollars. I'm talking about setting a modest financial goal that enables you to get by and manage, and which allows you to pursue your dream without major interruption. That's a critically important goal—there's no way around it.

Every aspect of family or personal financial management requires careful thought and planning if it is to be successful. You need to know where you want to go and devise the proper strategy to get there—particularly if your life's mission involves a change in your job or career, or a substantial reduction in income.

If you're unsure of your planning and strategy— if projected budgets don't seem to balance out, for example—you're likely to benefit from professional financial advice. As I said elsewhere in this book, none of us is as smart as all of us, and a knowledgeable third party can often spot potential problems and offer solutions that can spell the difference between financial stability and future crisis. Consulting a pro, even if you don't think you need to, is generally money well spent. It focuses us on real-life numbers, and that, in itself, is a solid learning experience for anyone.

Among the general rules for financial stability, there is one that I put at the head of the list: get professional tax advice if you're not positive you know what you're doing. The consequences of not doing things right can lead to weeks, months, even years of time-consuming aggravation. It's not worth it.

Protecting your credit ranks Number 2 on my list of financial rules. Failing to make timely payments on bank loans, credit cards, and auto and equipment purchases—anything for which you've contracted—can come back to haunt you big-time. It can ruin your credit rating, and you might find it impossible to buy anything on time. And I mean anything—houses, cars, appliances, furniture, and everything else. You don't want that to happen to you.

The best way to avoid a bad credit rating is to borrow responsibly—no more than you know you can pay back on time. It takes firm discipline, and we've got a nation full of people who don't exercise it. The problem has become so widespread that magazines and newspapers are filled with self-help articles advising readers on the dangers of excessive borrowing and suggesting various ways to budget and get their debt under control.

Many states and communities have set up official agencies to help delinquent borrowers and save them from bankruptcy and a ruined credit rating. Often, this help involves the arranging of meetings between the borrower and the bank or other suppliers—in the hope that they'll rewrite payment schedules to fit the debtor's budget. Sometimes it works out. Sometimes it doesn't. And you can imagine how embarrassing it is for the borrower.

It can all be avoided, of course, by spending less than you make. Sounds simple, doesn't it? It's common sense. But we live in a society of boundless merchandise, easy credit, and immense temptation—a place where frugality, common sense, and balanced budgets are rarer than unicorns. (Our own federal government is the pre-eminent example of over-borrowing and over-spending.)

Protecting your credit is up to you and the discipline you and your family can exercise. Like everything else involving money, the problem with failing to manage it sensibly and keeping your spending within bounds is that it has long-range effects on everything you dream of doing in the future. That's where I'm focused. And I believe that's where you're focused. For many people, however, overspending on material things now is more important than preserving their good credit for the future. Their priority is instant gratification.

It's just the opposite for people who have a mission in life and who are determined to achieve it.

My Dad always told my brothers and me to pay ten percent of our income to ourselves. In other words, tithe to ourselves—pay ourselves first. If it's part of your belief system to tithe to your Maker, then give yourself the second ten percent. It's sound advice. Put it in your savings account. Or invest it.

One investment idea you might consider is buying stock in the company you work for, if you plan to stay there. Stock gives you an ownership stake, improves your job performance, and puts your superiors on notice that you have faith in the company and a serious interest in its progress—not a bad impression to make on management executives.

Or you can salt your self-tithe away in an Individual Retirement Account (IRA). The younger you start an IRA, the better. The tax-deferred savings accumulation can be amazing! Get the figures from your bank; you'll be astounded.

However you pay yourself, the point is to <u>do</u> it and build up equity cushions—a short-range cushion (such as a savings account) for unexpected emergencies, vacations, planned projects, etc., and a long-range cushion (such as an IRA) for use in the future when your income will probably be substantially less than it is today.

Paying yourself is a habit. Once you start, it becomes addictive. If you can't afford ten per cent of your income, make it less. I believe that <u>everybody</u>—even the poorest of us—can systematically put away <u>something</u>.

One thing you don't want to do is keep your savings at home. First of all, it's not safe—and second, you'll be tempted to dig into them. Put your money into an investment, a bank, a mutual fund, or whatever—just get it out of sight and keep adding to it faithfully. When you look at the increasing balance in your passbook or on your periodic statement, you'll find yourself trying to figure out ways to make it grow faster. It happens. It's addictive—and it's the right kind of addiction.

Finally, I'm sure every reader fully understands the family and relationship stresses that can be caused by financial troubles.

Solid relationships—in which there is mutual respect and trust, unconditional love, and good communication—won't break up simply because of lack of money. But if there's been little financial planning and responsibility—if that's the cause of the financial troubles that have cropped up—then even the best relationship can be severely stressed. It's uncomfortable. It's unpleasant. And above all, it's unnecessary.

I say it again—*you're better than that!*

By seriously paying attention to money matters ... by exercising the common sense and discipline that enable you to avoid unwarranted financial crises ... by responsibly doing the best with what little you may have ... money-connected stress can be reduced to a minimum. And it's very important that everybody in the relationship knows what's going on ... that the best is being done. They should know the goals for which sacrifices are being made. This establishes the common-cause atmosphere in which relationships thrive.

The substance of everything I've said in this chapter about financial management really boils down to three things: Common sense. Discipline. And caring—caring enough to exercise that common sense and discipline. That's what it's about, and you know it.

Remember, <u>to know and not do is not to know</u>. That's not the way for you. I believe you'll decide today, January 1st, to keep your financial house in order. You'll do what you know—for the sake of your dream, for the sake of your relationships, and for the sake of winning where countless others needlessly fail.

Never will you do so little to accomplish so much. Fiscal fitness is one of the most important winner's edges you can give yourself.

No more excuses.

<u>Decide</u>!

12

THE WATER OF LIFE

In Chapter Nine, you'll recall I presented my audience with a bowl that was filled to the brim with marbles. There was obviously no room in the bowl for anything else. But then I was able to pour a whole box of salt into the bowl. And then a pitcher of water.

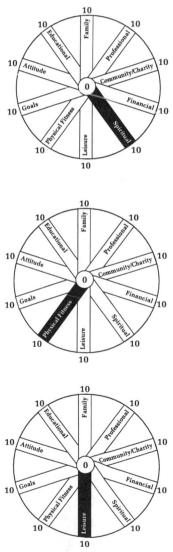

The point was to show that no matter how filled up your day might be, there's always room left to fit in other important priorities. The marbles represent your work schedule. The salt represents family and relationship priorities. The water was the last thing put into the bowl, but it ranks among the most important. I think of it as the "Water of Life"—and it represents three of the most essential spokes in the Circle of Life—*the spiritual, physical fitness*, and *leisure* priorities.

I believe that we all must make room for the Water of Life

in our daily lives if we are to balance out the other spokes. These are the three essential priorities that help meld our families together in good times and bad; that increase our feelings of well-being and optimism; that enable us to work better, think better, and live more enjoyably.

These are the three priorities that quietly and steadily support our spirit, enabling us to put our *permission to win* into action. They are that important—that real—and it's fitting for me to save them for the end in completing the Circle of Life. This is where the circle starts and ends.

I have to pause here to take my mask off and say a few things. Writing this book has been the single most difficult task I've ever undertaken. For years, I've dreamed of the day I'd be finished with this manuscript and asking everyone to read it. However, I never dreamed that the person who needed to read this book the most would be its author.

I need the coaching I'm giving you. I feel like a preacher who still lusts, or who is tempted and falls. Who is Ray Pelletier to talk about spiritual matters or physical fitness or, even, for that matter, financial affairs? I haven't mastered any of them. I'm afraid someone in my family or a friend at my breakfast club will say, *"Practice what you preach, Ray!"* My frequent prayer is that my life catches up with my mouth.

I'm a fellow struggler. Although I readily forgive others who trespass against me, and will be writing about forgiveness in a moment, I don't pray as often as I should or tend to all of my other spiritual needs. I've worked hard at physical fitness, losing 193 pounds at one time, yet I put a hundred of it back on. I don't walk and exercise _every_ day. I don't eat right every day. But I know what to do, and I'm improving. I'm working at this thing called life.

Be patient with me. I have to be patient with myself. You have to be patient with yourself. God's not through molding us. He's not done with us yet. Be patient. It's one day at a time.

Those things needed to be said.

Spiritual

Among the readers of this book are people of many different faiths. Some readers aren't affiliated with any faith and are still searching for spiritual and philosophical anchors.

"Spiritual," as I use it, does not refer to your formal religion (or lack of it), but to the way you respond to the ever-present inner influences common to all of us within our spirit—our innate sense of right and wrong, decency, honesty, fairness, forgiveness, love for our neighbors, and compassion. We're all aware of being inwardly called upon in some degree to practice these things whether we believe in God or not. Some call it conscience. Some embrace it. Some ignore it—or try to. But those who give themselves _permission to win_ pay attention to it with a passion.

Faith and conscience exert an irresistible influence on our lives. We are never so aware of our doings as when we are at odds with these deepest of all forces within ourselves. When we resist these forces, those of us who believe in God are aware that they're failing Him; those who don't believe in God are aware they're failing themselves. Self-esteem is decreased. We don't like ourselves very much. We are uneasy with what we've done or not done. Feelings like these have a subtly destructive effect on our winner's attitude, our relationships, our careers, and everything else in our lives.

We're better than that! All of us are.

Let's start with forgiveness.

A basic requirement of *permission to win* is to forgive yourself for your past mistakes. Start over and get on with winning.

A second requirement is to forgive others.

In both cases, we're talking about burying yesterday. It's gone. It's unwelcome baggage.

Resentments, thoughts of revenge, obsessing over past failures and disappointments ... all of this will slow you down, occupy your mind with negatives, and stand immovably in the way of your progress, fulfillment, and inner peace.

The way to avoid it is simple: forgive.

To forgive others is good for us. It frees us of all those negatives I just mentioned. At one time or another, everyone reading this book has struggled to forgive someone—we all have, and sometimes it can be tough. But we <u>know</u> it's the right thing to do. And those of us who have accomplished it know how it releases us. It's probably the most spiritually satisfying thing a person can do.

When you give yourself *permission to win,* forgiving gradually becomes instinctive, even automatic; it's seen as an <u>opportunity</u> rather than a challenge. When you're falsely accused of something or otherwise given reason to bear a grudge against someone, you'll be aware that unless you forgive that person, <u>immediately and genuinely</u>, you'll be loading yourself down with lingering resentments and ill feelings that will fill your life with negatives.

You won't want to do that to yourself. Your winner's attitude won't allow it. You'll want to grasp the opportunity to save yourself from such negativity. And I speak from experience—you won't want any part of the problems caused by nursing bad feelings toward someone else. Since giving myself *permission to win,* forgiving has become a familiar pattern in my life, and the results have been priceless for my peace of mind and mental freedom.

You'll hear people say: *"Don't get mad ... get even."* That's the worst possible kind of coaching. It teaches you to carry revenge around in your thoughts. Don't fall for it. *You're better than that!* It's okay to get mad for a moment. But then get over it. Right then and there. Forgive. Forget. And then get on with your life.

Remember what some say of God—that He has a bad memory. He forgives and forgets our trespasses. And indeed He does if we respond to Him as He asks. In turn, forgiveness of others is one of the things He expects of us—it's a cardinal teaching passed down to us intact and preserved in the world's major religions despite whatever other doctrinal differences may have emerged. Name the religion and it's in there as a primary teaching.

Why? Because *forgiving is good for us!* To forgive others is our request to be forgiven. Whoever you are, whatever religious beliefs you may hold or not hold, your spiritual sense knows what I'm saying. You know it and you feel it. It's the right thing to do, and there is hope in it.

Resolving differences is somewhat like forgiving. When you have differences with another person, you need to resolve them immediately. When I was five years old, my Dad told me that men don't hug and men don't kiss. I really wish he hadn't said that—it kept me from telling him I loved him until he was on his deathbed. He was on that deathbed for a year, dying of cancer, and nearly every night during that year I drove two hours to that hospital from a town in another state to tell my Dad that I loved him.

The childhood programming he had given me was a tragedy—it was a terrible loss to me not to have been able to express my love for my father over all those many years. He gave me bad coaching, and I should have discussed and settled it with him years earlier—as soon as I was old enough to understand what he was denying me.

I made a vow during those hospital visits that whenever an important difference came up between myself and someone else I'd never again allow a day to pass without trying to settle it. Unresolved differences—like failing to forgive—can fester in our hearts and cause long-lasting resentments that occupy our thoughts and rob us of spiritual comfort. Scripture, philosophy, and psychological treatises are filled with admonitions to quickly resolve our differences with others and free ourselves of such negative distractions. Again—*it's good for us!*

And it's good for the other person.

Sometimes differences and misunderstandings exist in the mind of only one party—not both. When you settle things with that person, you're giving him or her a spiritual gift. You're freeing them of their own baggage.

I have a writer friend, Fred, who was two years old when his father took to drinking heavily and abandoned the family. For the next fifteen years, Fred hardly saw the man—only two times, as he recalls. And then only for a few minutes.

When Fred was eighteen, he was on his own. His mother had died, he had no close relatives, and he'd gone into business for himself. Somehow, he managed to locate his father and arranged for him to come up to the office for a visit.

His father arrived with a buddy he'd found somewhere in New York's skid row district and they all had a half-hour chat in the kid's office. It was friendly. Fred saw to it there was no awkwardness. No tightness. Just a general conversation and some easygoing catching-up on things. There was no malice in Fred. There was no resentment toward his father. He was a young man of genuine goodwill, enjoying life, able to take good care of himself, and blessed with a highly positive spirit.

But you can imagine what was going on in his father's mind. After fifteen years of doing his own thing and totally ignoring his child—and surely expecting a heavy scene and a merciless accounting of things—here he was being welcomed by that child, now mostly grown and showing not even the remotest sign of ill will. Not a word about accounting for anything. It was like nothing had ever happened.

When it was time for his father to leave, Fred gave him a hug. The father looked surprised and Fred said: *"Hey, you're my father."*

It was a long flight of stairs down to the street level and when Fred's father had left the building his buddy came back alone, walked up the stairs and said this: *"Fred, that was the most decent thing I've ever heard one man say to another. Your father is crying. You don't know what a fine thing you've done for that man."*

That's the story. Fred hadn't thought there was anything extraordinary in what he'd said to his father.

The man <u>was</u> his father. That was all there was to it. His thoughts were genuine. There was no guile. There was no other motive or design behind his words.

What the settling of differences can do for your own spiritual well-being is one thing. But, as in this story, what it can do for the other person's spiritual well-being can be beyond measuring.

Fred had an instinctive, irrepressible, solid-gold January 1st attitude—and he made a gift of it to his father.

And so can you—to the people in your life.

Think about it. Settle differences. Correct misunderstandings. Free each other of heaviness, regret and the terrible baggage that ruins countless lives. And start today.

"Love one another."

In this generation, many have fled from their spiritual values. They've fled from themselves and their deepest spiritual instincts. We live in a society of accusations and casting stones, of lives that don't match words, of obsession with comfortless material gain and amusement, of yearnings for status and power. If we took the time to think about it clearly, some of the most prominent people in our society are those whom we probably wouldn't allow into our living rooms.

Drug use, viciousness, hate, lust, greed, and unredressed crime are the new Commandments, replacing the originals which the world has found outmoded and naive. This is the large measure of our society—the society shaped by the movers and shakers who have the power to set the public tone and make it over in their own image.

There's nothing so rewarding as to make people realize they are worthwhile in this world.

— Bob Anderson, English poet

But it's not in the hearts of most of us. The image is superficial—a gaudy piece of wrapping paper around a huge package of good. There is a great and abiding decency in our society, and most of us stand aside in dismay at what is being forced upon us by a few. It is anathema to us. It's inherently, irrevocably wrong.

What can you do to change it? You can choose from among a thousand ways; there's no end to the political and social-action causes that would welcome your earnest participation.

But, above all, you can do this:

Tend to your spiritual self—listen to it and embrace it. This is where change starts in our society—with you. Never ignore or compromise the instinctive urgings of conscience; the inner understandings that plainly and emphatically define right from wrong in all your dealings; the urgings that turn your heart toward the spiritual welfare of your fellow humans so that you place no obstacles or temptations in their way; the urgings that insist you forgive and that insist you offer good will toward your neighbor and that insist you not judge others with narrow coldness, but rather, that you try to set things right and be the maker of peace.

Do that in your life, and you will begin to change our society. The personal blessings to yourself, to those you touch, and to our society can be extraordinary.

Physical fitness

Ask our senior citizens about the value of physical fitness. Ask those who didn't pay attention to health and nutrition in their younger years about the

---

What you are is God's gift to you, and what you do with what you are is your gift to God.

— George Foster, Major League outfielder

hard price they're paying for it now. Ask them about the incredible swiftness of time; listen carefully, be wise, look at it through their eyes, and understand that to be 60 or 70 today is to have been 25 only yesterday. It's that fast. What is it our elders say? *"Oh, to be young again!"*

Indeed, to be young again; to be able to go back and refuse that first cigarette, to eat more wisely, to exercise more regularly, to control stress. Indeed, were it possible for the senior generation to go back and start over with the wisdom they've gained about physical fitness, millions would totally reprogram their past lives.

Today, you have *permission to win* regarding health and physical fitness. You have given yourself permission to learn and to listen and to understand its value, and to do what it takes to give yourself the priceless gift of good health for the years ahead. Fate and genetics play a role—but insofar as it is within your power to direct your conditioning, you are in a position to arrange it.

It took a ruptured spleen to get me focused on health.

After having experienced pain so intense that I passed out, I was to lay in a hospital room for <u>thirty-four days</u> before the doctors could discover what was wrong with me. During that time, the only thing I could see from my window was a tree. Before I went into that hospital room, my mission was to touch the world with my message. Now my mission was far more simple and consuming; it was simply to touch that tree.

Lying on that hospital bed for all those weeks—completely vulnerable, frightened, confused, certain I was about to die—I understood for the first time the consummate value of life and good health. Never again was I to take my health—or my life—for granted. It was a life-changing experience in the truest sense of the term.

A few weeks after my hospital stay, I was speaking in California and decided to spend an extra day taking a Grey Line bus tour to Muir Woods, a redwood forest. I'd never done such a thing before—I had invariably taken a plane somewhere, done my speaking, and then come home, blind to the world around me. But not this time ... not after what I'd been through. It's said that to appreciate life we should stop and smell the roses. But I tell you I wanted to stop and smell not only the roses, but every weed and blade of grass.

Standing among the redwoods in a chilly rain, staring up to the top of the most majestic trees in existence, I was humbled and awestruck beyond anything I could have imagined. I was speechless. Overcome. It was a communion with the God who had just delivered me from death.

Nor was it to be lessened by the grumbling of some passengers who were complaining loudly about the rain. I wanted to shake them. I wanted to tell them to get on their knees and thank God that they were allowed to walk and breathe and be alive to see such a thing as this.

Those were the thoughts I had, and I'd never had such thoughts before. They were good thoughts, and I regretted only that it had taken a brush with death to bring me to my senses.

Too often in life, it takes an emergency—a sudden failing of health—to get our attention and focus us on the incomparable blessings of life and a sound body. And sometimes it comes too late. I was fortunate; I was smiled upon and given a second chance. Many people don't get a second chance.

The message is plain: now—today—understand what you must do for yourself. Tend to your health and nurture it as if it would fade tomorrow without your care. Because it can. Whether you're currently in good health or poor, struck down with disease or free of it, what you have is what you must work with, building up what conditioning you can. It's the foundation on which your future well-being will stand, and it takes time to build it strong. Ask the seniors. They'll tell you. Don't put it off. Don't wait. Don't be as I was ... with half my life lived before I understood.

Anybody can appreciate the value of physical fitness from a deathbed. I expect you to appreciate it from a life-bed.

Excessive weight and its destructive effects on the body are everywhere considered one of the biggest health problems in our society.

Losing weight has always been a challenge for me. In my younger days, when I was an athlete, I spent every waking hour I could on the football field, and it was easy for me to keep myself in shape. Once those days were over, however, my primary source of exercise was just carrying my excessive weight around. At one point I reached an astounding 418 pounds!

Following the wake-up call of thirty-four days in the hospital—which gave me a new appreciation of good health—I had no intention of succumbing to a heart attack because I couldn't keep my weight under control. So I went at the problem with a vengeance. This meant mind control—a positive, I will win attitude—and it meant daily exercise and dieting.

It was the biggest mountain I've ever had to climb, but by taking it one step at a time I started accomplishing big-time weight loss. What is it they say? *Inch by inch, anything's a cinch.* But that was a discipline I had to learn from experience. At first I'd expected a big miracle—from fatso to hunk in a few weeks. But I had to be patient and settle for a whole bunch of smaller miracles—pound by pound, day after day, month after month.

I can't say I was 100% successful. I still haven't reached my final destination, but it's within sight, and when I attain it it will rank among the biggest—and smartest—achievements of my life.

I don't stand alone in that assessment. Oprah Winfrey, and others who have gone through a major weight-loss experience, stand in awe at what they'vo achieved—not only for how it's improved their bodies and general health, but for how it's boosted their self-esteem and mental outlook. I'm talking about quantum leaps here, like going from one world into another. I know. I made the trip.

You can start that trip today. But remember, it begins in your head. The only thing standing in the way of losing weight is the <u>decision</u> to do it.

If you say you don't care, I don't believe you. (Everybody wants to look and feel better. You just haven't decided to pay the price.) Not caring is an excuse—and you don't make excuses anymore. That was December 31st. Not January 1st.

As a winner, you'll be processing things in a new way: <u>One</u>—you know that getting your weight under control is worth it from the cosmetic standpoint. <u>Two</u>—you know it's worth it from the self-esteem standpoint. And <u>three</u>—from the long-term health and physical fitness standpoint, you know it's worth it beyond any price you can name.

As a champion, you'll approach those worthwhile goals differently than you have in the past—you'll know you can achieve them if you <u>decide</u> to go for it. Every one of those objectives is worthy of championship effort—and reaching them is already a reality the moment you <u>decide</u> to accomplish them.

I believe you'll do that. I believe you'll do what I'm doing—you'll answer the wake-up call, appreciate the value of good health, and tackle your weight-control issue with a vengeance.

Please keep in mind that weight-control is a daily challenge for me. I feel like a hypocrite as I write this—a poor example of the advice I give. But by continuing to struggle, being patient with myself, and <u>deciding</u> to win I know I already have the victory. There's no hypocrisy in writing about the struggle. It is the most persistent struggle in my life, and will be among my life's greatest victories.

Now, I have to tell you a great, and very brief, little story:

Not too long ago, a little girl came up to me after an assembly. She put her head on my shoulder and gave me perhaps the greatest compliment I've ever received. She said: *"Coach, do you know why you're so big?"*

"No, sweetheart. Why?"

"It's to hold your heart."

Earlier in this book, I told you how I often try to fit in a walk before I start work, even a swim if possible, and how it prepares me not only physically for my day, but also mentally. It gives me a positive start.

Some would rather <u>run</u> in the morning, but it may not be good for their knees. It could do more harm than good. I know many doctors, especially through my sports connections, and I know it's best to listen to them about exercise. Pay attention to your doctor's advice, take exercise in small doses, and never overdo.

I pass that along because I know many of you will be determined to win and maintain good health, and I don't want anyone to push themselves too hard. A physical checkup by your doctor—and some words of advice—is the place to start.

One of the most dangerous and subtle killers is stress—and one of the best antidotes for stress and the toxins it appears to build up in the body is regular exercise. Having a bad day at the office? Try a little exercise after work. Uptight about a relationship? Walk or run it off. It's amazing what magic it can work. You'll feel alive. Refreshed. And while your body is replenished with vitality, so too is your mind.

I can't tell you how many times I've seen athletes arrive for training in a sour mood—worried about relationship problems, worried about performing, worried about everything, so stressed out they can hardly hold a civil conversation—only to snap out of it and change before my eyes as they start running around the field and get their blood pumping. Exercise is the athlete's "high"—the conqueror of stress. It truly is magic. Like waving a wand.

It's been said of stress that it's the number one reason people don't show up for work—stress headaches. The cost to corporations is staggering, not to mention the loss to those who aren't at work. Any way we can relieve stress in our lives will pay off with big dividends. Medical doctors, psychologists, coaches—all will tell you that regular exercise is among the best of those ways.

The exercise prescription applies to many common health issues. We simply don't take care of our bodies. We're in denial. We refuse to take off our masks and admit that we need to do something about our physical conditioning.

If your work is sedentary—sitting at a computer or desk all day—you have to make up for your lack of exercise. You can do it before work. Or you can do it after work. Or maybe during work breaks. There are even books and programs on the market that show you ways to mildly exercise <u>while</u> you work at your desk. The essential thing is to start focusing on your need for exercise. It has to be in your mind—a priority. Remember the bowl of marbles and salt and water—you <u>can</u> make room for it in your day.

Millions of people <u>know</u> they should start an exercise program. They talk about it. Swear they'll do it. Yet, they don't do it. They make excuses. And day by day they grow slower and stiffer and less physically fit. They sabotage their health, robbing themselves of the joys of good physical conditioning, denying themselves the privilege of leading less stressful lives in the present and the prospects of a far more enjoyable and carefree life in the future.

A man I know admits to not having exercised in several years. *"In the dunes,"* he told me, *"that's where I love to walk. Along the beaches and in the dunes."*

Yeah, well wouldn't we all. But there aren't any dunes or beaches where this man lives—just rocks and trees, and these don't turn him on. So he sits at a desk all day and works well into the night—and he knows (he tells me this) that his formerly healthy conditioning is deteriorating rapidly. He sees it in his legs and his upper body. His breathing has become labored when he climbs the stairs to his bedroom. He continues to smoke.

Yet, so blessed has he been with good health in the past that he's sure he can regain his conditioning at any time.

So, he hangs on to his excuses. This man is in a make-believe world. He's dreaming. If he doesn't get his sense back, his habits will cost him a terrible price in his later years. He's cheating himself big-time.

I've seen a lot of athletes cheat themselves. Do you know what a "loser's limp" is? Imagine a football game. The tight end goes running out and misses a perfect pass from the quarterback. The ball hits his hands and bounces off. Nobody has touched him. The pass was right on the numbers. Yet he misses it and falls down. At that point, he gets up and walks to the sidelines—with a limp.

Did he really get hurt? No. Not a bit. And a lot of his teammates suspect it. When he gets to the sidelines, he establishes eye contact with the coach and walks as if he's in great pain. Then he goes to the trainer and continues to milk his "injury" for all it's worth. I've seen this happen over and over again.

That player is cheating himself. He thinks he's getting away with it, but it will come back to haunt him in the future when the coach picks out his players or when his career is at stake and his performance is being evaluated.

Frankly, I've seen a lot of people go through life with a loser's limp—refusing to be a winner and to do what it takes to stay on top. When that includes physical fitness, the cost is particularly heavy down the road.

You don't want to owe that bill. And you know what you have to do to avoid it.

Exercise.

What kind of problem do you have? Admit it and ask for help. By taking off your mask—I promise you—you will reap the biggest benefit of your life.

"I NEED HELP" is one of the most powerful and productive phrases in the English language. But sometimes it takes courage to say it. If you need to say it, I believe you have that courage. You have given yourself *permission to win*. You have permission to be honest with yourself, to be unafraid, to do what you must do to win the victories you need to win. You have permission to say those words: "I NEED HELP."

Admit that you need a coach in your life. If you want to be a better hitter, you go to a batting instructor. If you want to understand your taxes, you go to a tax advisor. I have several coaches in my own life. I'm not embarrassed to go to them. I <u>need</u> them so I can be better in certain areas of my work. I <u>expect to win</u>—and when I need help, I ask for it.

In my seminars I often ask the audience to tell me the biggest problems they have in their lives, both at work and at home. I don't ask them to state them publicly, but to write their answers on cards. They don't have to sign the cards, so privacy is assured. This way, I know I'll mostly get dead-honest answers.

In reviewing those cards, I found that serious health problems—both mental and physical—rank among the top two or three concerns. Some of the respondents have AIDS or cancer or substance-abuse problems. Many are seriously depressed. Their co-workers and bosses don't know about it. Nobody knows about it. They're embarrassed to talk about it; afraid they might be disliked or lose their jobs. They don't feel safe taking off their masks.

In some cases, they're right. They might risk losing their jobs. Unfortunately, in some companies, the executives are so shallow that they look at these problems as a negative rather than facing them head-on and pitching in to help. That puts employees in a tough position. They want to give the company their best, but can't unless they're up-front and ask the company for help. But if they expose their problems, they know they'll be fired. It's a Catch-22.

Everybody loses in that situation—and it's the company that loses the most. If it doesn't have the full trust and confidence of its employees, it's undermining itself. Sure, by keeping quiet an employee can keep his or her job and get by with doing work that is obviously satisfactory to the company. But how much <u>better</u> that employee would be for the company if he or she were getting medical or psychological help from management! You'd be amazed how many corporate executives can't see it that way.

But you'd be equally amazed at how many other corporate executives have seen the light.

What's my point? It's this: If you don't get help because you don't trust your company, that's just an excuse. And *you're better than that!* If you feel you can't ask your company for help, then ask for help elsewhere. Go to a professional in your community—get medical help or substance abuse counseling—whatever it is you know you need.

If you can't afford private help, call your state's Human Services Department (or comparable agency). They'll direct you to local state (or county) offices or clinics where you can get the assistance you need at little or no cost—and where your privacy should be protected. And remember to check your local newspaper's classified section. You should find listings there for Alcoholics Anonymous, cancer support groups, and similar no-cost self-help programs. One of them might be exactly what you're looking for.

"I NEED HELP." Those are the words. And that's the message.

They're the words of a winner—of someone not afraid or embarrassed to win ... of someone who <u>will</u> <u>not</u> allow their problems to control and ruin their life.

Good nutrition—the careful and sensible selection of foods—is essential to maintaining good health and physical fitness. And never has there been so much publicity about it as there is now.

My soul-mate, Joyce, has the best eating habits I've ever seen. She's so wise! She knows how to control herself. She eats the right foods in the right proportions, and she exercises every day to get the full benefit of proper nutrition. When I grow up, I want to eat like she does!

Ours is a fast-food, prepared-food, junk-food society. It goes with the system. Millions of single-parent families, or families where both parents work, have little time to shop properly or cook wholesome meals. And when they do shop, what do they find? Store shelves filled with packaged meals and foods that have been refined, bleached, over-salted, over-sugared, and over-processed in so many ways that they've been robbed of most of their natural nutrients and fibers and have more in common with a chemistry lab than a farm.

It's a big game, this food business. It's played with Nature. To make food more attractive and less perishable, they take the real stuff out and put the fake stuff in. When they strip wheat of its bran, for example, they might make it more palatable and saleable, such as with most popular white breads and cereals, but the oils, fiber, and nutrition of the bran and whole wheat are gone. So they add vitamins made in a lab. What do you think is better for you? The way God made it? Or the way they made it?

They take the odor out of garlic, one of the truly great foods with highly praised nutritional benefits. *But who's to say that the odor, itself, isn't one of the reasons garlic works so many healthful wonders in our body?*

Every day, new discoveries are being made about the foods we eat, and almost invariably it has to do with the "surprising" benefits of these foods in their natural state.

Improving your nutrition is—once again—a matter of deciding. Basically, it's a decision to be conscious of nutrition. With that decision comes a constant awareness of what you're putting into your body—and into the bodies of your family.

Make that decision, and you'll find yourself doing a few new things. You'll start noticing articles on nutrition—and reading them. You'll begin to learn more. You'll read labels more carefully. You'll stay away from saturated fats. You'll cut way down on junk food. You'll eat less meat, and more vegetables, fruits, and whole-wheat products. And if you have to buy prepared meals, you'll be more selective and more likely to buy those that have been processed with your good health in mind.

It's a learning process. As you progress, you'll start asking yourself if the fruits and vegetables you buy have been organically grown (without chemical fertilizers). They're more expensive and sometimes hard to find, but that's what you'll start to prefer. You'll look at the "Natural Foods" section of your supermarket with new interest. You'll hesitate to buy pastries and other highly-processed foods, such as nitrate-filled luncheon meats. You'll find yourself making fewer stops at fast-food restaurants (or at least you'll choose what you order more carefully). You'll bring home more fruit juices than sodas.

When you make the decision to be conscious of nutrition, all of these new thoughts start to take hold. It becomes a habit. A good one.

So decide—put your winner's mind on it—and you'll take the basic and most necessary step toward good nutrition for you and your family.

The rest will come naturally through your ever-increasing interest.

Leisure

Chilling out ... taking time off ... doing what you like to do ... tending to hobbies ... whatever it is, leisure is a vital part of *permission to win.* You have permission to do nothing.

Ain't it great!

Leisure and exercise often go together. For some, it can be the same thing—such as taking a long walk or a swim or a bike ride—and they have similar effects on stress. But mostly, leisure means pampering yourself and collecting your thoughts, smelling the roses and enjoying life. Leisure is having <u>fun</u>.

I think leisure is so important that I try to schedule it—like a business appointment. If you're as busy as I am, you might have to do the same thing. My trip to the redwood forest was leisure. I hadn't scheduled it at the time, but today I usually keep my eye on my daily planner to see where I can fit in a day of doing something just for the fun of it.

I think one reason people don't take more time for leisure is because they're insecure. They're afraid they'll lose what they have, so they work very hard to keep it. Leisure time is seen as wasted time. I know these feelings. I've had to struggle with them myself since childhood, and even today I sometimes feel a twinge of guilt when I deliberately put my work aside and concentrate on having some fun.

But the truth of the matter is that I'm <u>better</u> at my work—and can do it faster and more efficiently— when I schedule in regular periods of leisure. Like exercise, leisure clears my head of cobwebs and gives me new vitality and a sense of well-being that improves my thinking and performance.

It's good stuff, leisure. Winner's stuff. Work it into your life.

Listening to your spiritual self ... maintaining good health ... exercising ... dieting, if necessary ... getting help when you need it ... paying attention to nutrition ... taking it easy and having fun on a regular basis ... all of these combine to complete the last spokes in the Circle of Life.

The last spokes, but by no means the least.

In some ways, perhaps the most important spokes of all.

PERMISSION TO WIN

"What fools we mortals be." Puck, a mischievous sprite in English folklore, probably said it best.

And we're all included.

We all make mistakes and mishandle ourselves. We can misinterpret and misunderstand and carry out one foolishness after another. We can be inept in our most important relationships. We can focus on a problem, analyze it in every detail, come to exactly the wrong conclusion, and then defend our position like a lion.

Sometimes, we have tunnel vision. We close ourselves off in our own small world of interest as if it were the universe—oblivious to all the learning, expertise, ideas, and willing help available to us on every hand just for the asking. In our blindness and stubborn self-containment, we can make life infinitely more complicated for ourselves.

And then, if we let our foolishness and incompetencies get to us, we load ourselves down with tons of negative baggage—regret, remorse, wishing we could go back and change things, filling ourselves up with self-pity and convictions of worthlessness. Probably 90% of our fellow humans—maybe 99%—spend their lives in a December 31st world. Their reality is yesterday's reality, and they wander around in it as if in a prison cell, as convinced as Houdini was that there is no way out.

And yet the cell door isn't locked. It's all in their minds.

Freeing ourselves of self-imposed restrictions and opening our minds to our champion's potential is what *permission to win* is all about. The moment we give ourselves *permission to win,* we walk out of the cells in which we've confined ourselves.

And yes, our restrictions <u>are</u> self-imposed. It <u>is</u> all in the mind. Attitude <u>is</u> everything!

Wherever your attitude takes you, that's where you are.

Cancer defeats the body—but your attitude can defeat cancer.

The loss of a career job can be the greatest downfall you ever suffered—or it can be the greatest opportunity of your life. It's attitude.

The breakup of a marriage or relationship can put a final, permanent end to your happiness, never again to be retrieved—or you can will your way back to emotional stability and an infinitely better situation in the future. Your attitude calls the play.

PERMISSION TO WIN turns fate upside down. Loss is victory. A negative is a positive.

PERMISSION TO WIN sends you forth on this planet not as a man or woman whose success or failure, misery or happiness, is subject to every whim of circumstance, but as a confident, positive, rare species of human with an <u>indomitable will to overcome</u>.

PERMISSION TO WIN is a solid-gold January 1st attitude toward every obstacle that life, society, and the demons of this world have designed for your destruction.

And I believe you have that attitude. I believe that as you finish this book you're embracing *permission to win* as you've never embraced anything like it before.

I believe you realize that <u>not</u> to embrace it is unthinkable.

So, now is the time—the time to go the mirror. It's the time to face yourself and confirm that you have given yourself *permission to win.*

Just do it. And say it: *"I give you permission to win."*

Sound silly? Trivial? Don't be so sure.

The mind is a surprising instrument. When you stand in front of that mirror speaking those words, it will become a firm memory that will jump out at you in supportive ways for the rest of your life. When a problem arises, when negativism rears up, you'll never forget being told face-to-face that you have permission to win and overcome.

There's tremendous power in that memory. Tremendous encouragement. Whatever your *opportunity to overcome* might be at the time, that simple recollection will push you toward approaching it in a more positive, competitive and confident manner. Winning will be on your mind—it can't help but be there. And that is the solution and the ultimate tool to attaining victory in every area of your Circle of Life.

You'll be calling forth the champion inside yourself. And when that champion steps forward, so will the recognition of your mission and the clear path to its fulfillment—the path that leads to the realization of the most precious of all blessings ... inner peace.

Do it. Call up your champion. Decide! Today, turn that champion loose!

Gang, I love you all. Go for it!

Not to decide is to decide!

LEARNING RESOURCES ARE AVAILABLE FROM RAY PELLETIER AND THE PELLETIER GROUP:

It has been said of Ray Pelletier, that when he speaks he is *"electrifying ... a new breed of speaker with an extraordinary ability to enthrall an audience with his message and reach them on deep, personal levels seldom achieved in this business. He speaks WITH his audiences, rather than TO them. He is one with them, and it is little wonder that a huge proportion of his speaking engagements are due to return requests."*

FOR PRODUCT AND ORDERING INFORMATION, PLEASE CALL

1-800-SPEAKER

OR WRITE TO:

RAY PELLETIER
THE PELLETIER GROUP
P.O. BOX 5411
MIAMI LAKES, FLORIDA 33014-1411